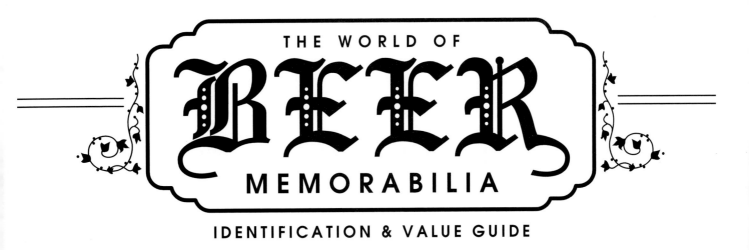

THE WORLD OF
BEER
MEMORABILIA
IDENTIFICATION & VALUE GUIDE

Herbert A. and Helen I. Haydock

COLLECTOR BOOKS
A Division of Schroeder Publishing Co., Inc.

The current values in this book should be used only as a guide. They are not intended to set prices, which vary from one section of the country to another. Auction prices as well as dealer prices vary greatly and are affected by condition as well as demand. Neither the Authors nor the Publisher assumes responsibility for any losses that might be incurred as a result of consulting this guide.

Searching for a Publisher?

We are always looking for knowledgeable people considered to be experts within their fields. If you feel that there is a real need for a book on your collectible subject and have a large comprehensive collection, contact Collector Books.

On the Cover:
Top left: Eberhardt & Ober Brewing Company poster, 44" x 28", $975.00.
Top right: Falstaff Brewing Company statue, 21", $350.00.
Center: Mabel Black Label, Carling Brewing Company barn, 23" x 26", $250.00.
Bottom left: Miller Brewing Company circular charger, NPA.
Bottom right: Joseph Schlitz Brewing Company double-sided sign, 23" x 19½", $1,200.00 – 1,400.00.

On Title Page:
Cardboard sign of Lewisburg Brewery. Lang & Knoll's Lager Beer Brewery, Covington, KY, 26" x 20".

On Contents Page:
Top: Lebanon Brewing Company reverse glass corner sign, 16" x 24", $1,200.00 – 1,400.00.
Center: Dubuque Brewing & Malting Company circular tray, 12½", $450.00 – 600.00.
Bottom: C. Gerhardt paper sign, 14" x 19", $600.00 – 800.00.

Layout and Design by:
Dave Turner
Turner Publishing Company
Paducah, Kentucky 42001

Additional copies of this book may be ordered from:

COLLECTOR BOOKS
P.O. Box 3009
Paducah, Kentucky 42002–3009

@ $24.95. Add $2.00 for postage and handling.

Copyright: Herbert A. and Helen I. Haydock, 1997

CONTENTS

Haydock Collection Display

DEDICATION

This book is dedicated to all the brewers from the **1800**s through the present. They have and are still playing an important part in the history of our country and their communities, where they were active in charitable and municipal affairs.

All of the brewers that we have had the opportunity to meet have always continued to offer the hospitality that was extended by their predecessors. A few of these brewers that hold a special place in our memories are the late Joseph Huber, Phil Shibilski, and Adolph Schumacher.

The Adam Schumacher Brewery began operations in **1886** and changed its name to Potosi Brewing Company in **1905**. It continued to brew beer until **1972**, when the president, Adolph Schumacher, decided to discontinue their operations.

Above: Adam Schumacher Brewery, 1890s. Back row, left to right: Mike Wright, Henry Watter, Frank Kadong, unidentified, Bill Kitto, unidentified, Adam S. Schumacher, Sr. Seated on ground: George Schumacher (brother of Nick and Adam) and George Schumacher who returned to Germany.

Opposite page: Large wood carved sign. A. Schumacher's, Potosi. Hand carved with American flags on both sides. Used outside Brewery's Tavern at Brewery. Painted on both sides; projected out from Tavern.
Adam Schumacher Brewery, Potosi, WI
Copyright: 1886 – 1903.
Size: 24" x 40"

It was a sad day in Potosi when we purchased and removed the brew kettle top and the grant. It was now a reality to the residents of Potosi that the brewery would never produce beer again. Mr. Schumacher made the statement at this time that he thought we would do something to keep the name of this brewery alive. We are pleased that it has been possible for us to fulfill these wishes.

Many of the breweries and their owners may have passed from the scene and this earth, but through our efforts and those of fellow collectors, they are not forgotten. The evidence of their places in our history is available for others to enjoy.

ACKNOWLEDGMENTS

One of the things we have enjoyed most in our many years of collecting is the opportunity to meet so many wonderful people. We would like to thank a small number of these people here...

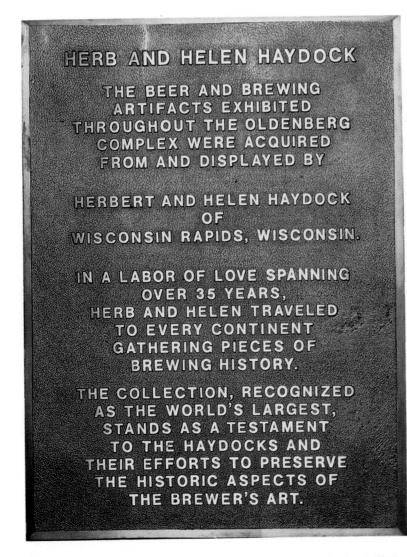

Our friend Jack Muzio permitted us to reprint the history of early advertising from his book *Collectible Tin Advertising Trays*. He saved us hours and hours of research.

Tom Hug, well-known dealer and collector of beer memorabilia, assisted us with the price guide. Norman Jay, an avid mug collector, assisted us with the pricing of the beer mugs.

Robert Gottschalk and Dale P. Van Wieren for all of their research and publishing of *American Breweries I and II.* We used their information throughout this book.

Without several years of persistence by Dave Turner, president of Turner Publishing Company, we probably would never have attempted to have this book published. Dave had complete control of the layout and design of this book. We would like to thank Mr. Turner and Bill Schroeder of Schroeder Publishing Company, Inc., for making this book a reality.

The friendship of our fellow collectors is just as rewarding as finding more memorabilia. One of these friends is Bill Luers, who was always available when assistance was needed. Thanks for all of the help, Bill!

Last, but not least, thanks to all of our relatives and friends in Wisconsin, for living with the collection through our lives. Special thanks go to our nieces and nephews for joining us on our collecting safaris.

Left: Helen and Herb Haydock in front of one of their many displays.

Above: Bronze plaque as displayed in the Oldenberg Brewery for the past eight years.

Notice the Potosi Beer sign on top of the bar, sixth from left. It is featured on page 131.

INTRODUCTION

In 1951, while Herb served as a cryptographer with the US Air Force in Munich, Germany, he purchased his first pieces of beer memorabilia: eight beer glasses. We didn't know it yet, but this small purchase would lead to us having the largest private collection of beer memorabilia in the world.

After returning home to Wisconsin Rapids, Wisconsin, we began collecting beer bottles, then trays, and finally everything with the name of a beer or brewery on it. We searched for memorabilia at flea markets, antique shops, advertising shows, and collectibles magazines, following any clue that might lead us to another object for our collection.

Our hobby has taken us to every continent in search of new artifacts. It wasn't unusual for us to leave our home in Wisconsin on Friday afternoon, drive to Adamstown, Pennsylvania, to visit the flea markets, then drive home on Monday. While traveling on vacation we would have to stop to ship memorabilia back to Wisconsin. On occasion the car was so full Herb threatened to make me ride on the fender or find another way home!

We soon discovered many other collectors with interests similar to ours. The East Coast Breweriana Association was the first club we joined. In 1972 Herb and two other collectors, Richard Bucht and John Murray, founded the National Association of Breweriana Advertising. He has been an officer and director of this organization since its founding. Herb also belongs to the American Breweriana Association, Beer Can Collectors of America, and many local chapters and collector clubs worldwide.

Many years and many miles later, we were ready to retire from our jobs. Herb worked for Consolidated Papers of Wisconsin Rapids for 39 years; I taught school for 34 years. Being avid travelers, and knowing that retirement would bring greater freedom to "see the world," our decision was made. By this time, the collection had grown to massive proportions; we stored it in every available space: home, garage, basement, patio....

The collection and its protection began to propose a dilemma: we wanted to share this part of American history with others rather than leaving it in storage.

We realized we needed to find a new home for it, and the search was on!

We entertained several offers from breweries, museums, etc., but these offers were usually only for certain portions of the collection, not the collection as a whole. The world's largest such collection, it represented over 34 years of our time and effort; to us, breaking up the collection would be like breaking up a family.

In 1985, while reading a beer trade journal, we ran across an article about the Oldenberg Brewery Project in Fort Mitchell, Kentucky. The scope and the uniqueness of Oldenberg sparked our interest, and we contacted Jerry Deters, Oldenberg's owner and developer. From our first conversation, we knew we were dealing with someone who shared our love of the history of beer and brewing. We were given a wonderful opportunity to display half of the collection in a beautiful showplace and pay tribute to the brewing traditions of the world.

After eight years, we realized Mr. Deters was preparing for retirement, and would not be building additional museum space. We continued our search for a facility where the entire collection could be displayed.

On January 22, 1996, the Miller Brewing Company provided this opportunity when they purchased the collection from us. The collection filled three Allied moving vans, and was returned to Wisconsin for display purposes to be determined.

Every object pictured in this book is either in the collection purchased by Miller, or in our private collection. Yes, we continue to collect; after all, as they say, once a collector, always a collector!

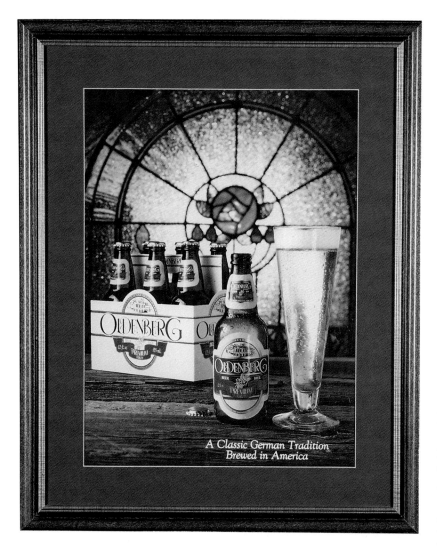

At right: Notice the Oshkosh Beer sign.

Below: An early example of advertising of Pilsener Beer. Three different examples displayed: round metal, corner porcelain, and a large canvas painted sign.

Opposite page, top: This bar scene shows many examples of advertising — the Pabst sign, Diebolt sign, calendar, trays, and murals. This is a scene many of we collectors have dreams of finding.

Opposite page, bottom: Long before the public observed brewery trucks traveling along the highways emblazed with colorful advertisements, the breweries used horse-drawn beerwagons with the cases displaying the name of the beer. A grand sight of the "good old days." There are collectors of these great old wooden cases.

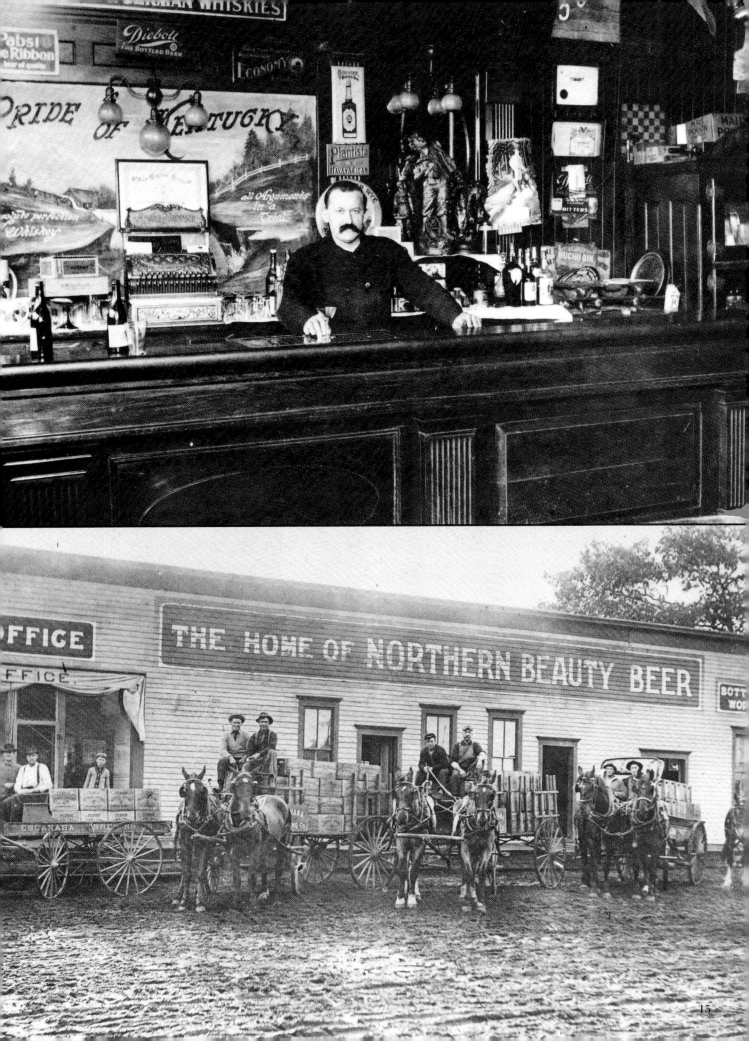

Albuquerque, NM, saloon, circa 1885.
Note the corner porcelain beer and the
flat Anheuser-Busch Lager Beer sign.

EARLY HISTORY

The history of tin advertising begins in the 1880s in the small town of Coshocton, Ohio. The industry was known then, and now, as the advertising specialty trade, or briefly, novelty advertising. Novelty advertising was born out of the concept of two competing pioneer Coshocton newspapermen, J.F. Meek and H.D. Beach. A third man, William Shaw, a local printer, is occasionally credited with being a forerunner in this type of advertising.

In the late 1880s William Shaw was printing ads on lithographed picture cards, called advertising or trade cards. These attractive advertising media were sold to local merchants, who in turn gave them to their customers. This was a very important aspect of early advertising. Trade cards were collected and pasted in albums by the thousands. Fortunately, they have again found their places as desirable collectibles.

In 1887 J.F. Meek conceived the idea of printing colorful ads on burlap school bags. This new idea in advertising was an immediate success and the afore-mentioned Mr. Shaw was employed as a part-time road salesman for Meek. Other advertising novelties were quickly added to their line, including lawn seats, backs of chairs (both porcelain and wood), umbrellas, fans, newspapers bags, grocery aprons...anything that could receive print satisfactorily was a potential advertising media. Meek called his new enterprise The Tuscarora Advertising Company, named after one of the rivers that flows near the town of Coshocton.

In 1888 H.D. Beach entered the novelty advertising field, organizing The Standard Advertising Company. He was also a Coshocton newspaper publisher, but of a rival paper, *The Democrat*. Beach's first specialty was reputed to have been the oilcloth school bag made of gum muslin. For several years he enjoyed virtually no competition in this line from his chief competitor (Meek simply did not know where to buy the much needed gum muslin) and H.D. Beach became firmly entrenched in the novelty advertising business.

In a town as small as Coshocton one might speculate that there wouldn't have been enough business for two growing firms of this type to succeed. To the contrary, there existed a ready nationwide market (not excluding

Novelty advertising.
Watch fob, Ritter Brau
Hastings Brewing Co., Hastings, NE
Brewery: 1908 – 1917
Size: 1¼" x 5"

Pocket watch,
Consumers Brewing Company of New York
Brewery: 1893 – 1928

Mexico) for these novelty items. Catalogs offering a varied selection of advertising novelties were issued, and well-dressed men in bowler hats were employed as salesmen. Business was good! New lines were added including rulers, basswood yardsticks, cloth caps, marble bags, wooden, metal, and paper calendars, thermometers, memoranda books. (All items that couldn't go through the presses were hand stenciled.)

The Standard Advertising Company's specialty was the art of placing ads on metal, although the Tuscarora Company had a similar process. These metal signs were first manufactured from the company's inception in **1889**. The art of printing gum engraved lithograph signs on metal was in its infancy. Little had been produced in this country, although there had been experimentation in other areas, notably Germany. In **1889** Mr. Shaw left The Tuscarora Company to join the Standard Company where he became a full-time salesman. Through his efforts he was to bring this firm into the forefront of the metal sign business. Mr. Beach was able to purchase black enamel plates, and tried printing signs directly from type. A small order was obtained by Shaw, but Beach found it impossible to print on this enameled metal. Beach had a decision to make: get out of this phase of the business, or look for an alternate method of printing on metal. Fortunately, his choice was to improve the process he was then using. He contacted the Ronemous Company of Baltimore, an early lithographer, and secured two men who were engaged in making metal signs from gum plates. (This process was invented in **1796** by Senefelder, a German artist.) Together, these men helped Beach considerably, and he was able to develop a steady art metal sign specialty business.

In **1890** or **1891**, Beach began using steam power presses, which according to a study by *Business Promotion* was "the earliest printing on metal done by power presses." Two other companies, The Shonk Company of Chicago, and the Ronemous Company of Baltimore also used power presses very early. However, it is believed these two companies did not introduce the power press until **1892**.

The Tuscarora Company in **1896** finally succumbed to the metal phase of the lithography business, and became a strong competitor in the metal sign business. They began experimenting with printing on metal in **1895**, and devised another process of lithographic offset printing on metal. Accordingly, they were the first company in the United States to use this new method of printing on metal in a commercial way. You will find early trays and signs with the name Tuscarora on them. These date from **1895** to **1901**.

Self-framed tin sign. Bottle of beer and a lobster.
Miller Beer, Fred Miller Brewing, Milwaukee, WI
Brewery: 1888 – 1920
Size: 18" x 15"

In March of **1901**, the two rival Coshocton companies, Standard and Tuscarora, merged as the Meek and Beach Company. The industry continued to grow, but in October **1901** H.D. Beach withdrew, sold out his interest, and started his own firm, The H.D. Beach Company. Mr. Meek continued in business, changing the name in **1905** from the Meek and Beach Company to the Meek Company. This company prospered until **1909** when it was reorganized into the American Art Works Company, keeping its metal sign and tray business, and adding art calendars, celluloid and leather advertising specialties. In 1925 the metal phase of the business began using silk screen processes in order to print the trays and signs.

The American Art Works ceased operations in 1950, and the two large business buildings were torn down.

The H.D. Beach Company, now known as The Beach Company, is active in business today in Coshocton, Ohio, under the very able leadership of James Beach, the great-grandson of the founder.

The Process: Printing on Metal

In the early days of chromo-lithography on metal, printing was done by employing stones. These stones were coated with the necessary ink in order to make a print. They were very crude, and often the pictures were of poor quality. To transfer ink from a stone and then to metal was almost an impossible task, the problem being that the metal was not smooth enough, and had too many variations of thicknesses. The Tuscarora Company (Meek) was foremost in its concern with this. The print was readable, but the picture was not clear enough for mass advertising. Meek finally devised a special part, built by a local firm, Keagy & Lear. It was a top cylinder, used for carrying a piece of rubber, onto which ink impressions from the stones were passed from the rubber-covered cylinder onto the metal. It proved a success, and in 1896 the first two firms ordering these new types of metal signs were Pettyjohn's Breakfast Food, and Sapolio, a cleansing soap company.

The following is the complete process of manufacture of advertising trays. It will take you back to the early phase of this business and explain in simplest detail the methods used by the Tuscarora and Standard Companies, then explain the process as it was improved upon up to the 1950s.

Trays from the 1890s to the 1920s were manufactured on flatbed offset lithograph presses. They were printed from limestone offset plates. (These limestone plates were obtained from Germany.) It was necessary for an artist to hand draw in lithographic crayon the several plates for each color and design that was desired on

Montage Collection. Tip tray with lithographic stone that was used to make print.
Hussa Brewing Company
Brewery: 1895 – 1920
Size: Tray – 4¼"

the tray or sign. In other words, if a tray had **14** colors or shades of designs in a pattern, it was necessary for the artist to break each color down into a different limestone plate; it would then be placed on the press and each color would involve one press run, totaling **14** press runs. It was not uncommon for a tray to have **20** press runs in order to get the desired color-tone or design in the original drawing duplicated on the tray. (On practice runs a design would be printed on a heavy card or piece of paper so that the process could be checked for errors.)

The early presses were known as offset presses. This meant the lithographic stone was placed in the bed of a press that moved in a horizontal motion. The ink rollers on the press would ink the plate (stone), and then the impression would be transferred to a cylinder that had a rubber piece wrapped around it. This rubber cylinder would then transfer the image or design to the metal piece (tray) as it passed through the press. It was then necessary to "rack" each piece of metal in a drying rack until it was completely dry. This process of printing and drying was used for each color! That is, the piece of metal was taken out of the drying rack, run through the press again (for another color), placed on the drying rack, dried, etc., until all of the desired colors were imprinted in a design on the metal.

After all the colors had been printed and dried, the metal sheet was run through a machine that coated it with clear varnish, protecting the design and the ink. The metal sheets were then taken to a press called a stamping die press which stamped out the shape and/or size of the tray. The tray was then transferred to the drawing presses where the lip of the tray was formed, and then transferred to still another press which curled the edge of the tray. A separate operation was needed for each bend in the tray. This was a tedious, expensive operation and yet, there were literally thousands of trays manufactured in this manner around the turn of the century.

Photolithography (the four-color process) was originated during the period between **1900** and **1910**. The original artist's drawing was photographed, each color being separated by a photographic process, and a dot-etch pattern formed on each plate (stone). This method was much faster, and by the different tones or shades of

Oval tray. Victorian lady standing.
ABC Brand. The American Brewing
Company, St. Louis, MO
Brewery: 1890 – 1906
Size: 14" x 17"

the pattern in the plate, any shade or design could be incorporated with only four press runs.

Originally the four-color process was used on the lithographic stone and the same process was used for printing. Because it took only four press runs, an artist's handwork on stone was soon eliminated. The lithograph stones were soon discarded in favor of the more accurate zinc plates. The same process was used in going through the press as before, except a zinc plate was used in place of a stone. This reduction of the passes through the press resulted in reduced drying time.

In later years it was discovered the zinc plate could be curved to fit a cylinder instead of a flat plane, resulting in faster production. It was necessary for the cylinder to turn twice for each movement of the reciprocating bed of the press. Today these presses attain a speed of from **4,000** to **10,000** impressions per hour. In the early days of the offset press they were lucky to get **1,000** impressions per hour.

The trades involved in the early days of novelty advertising were many and varied. Included were artists, lettering artists, stipplers, crayon artists, half tone artists, and the stone grinder, who prepared the stone and placed the wanted grain on the surface. Additionally, the transfer (who actually transferred the artist's original reproduction) put it all together, pulled impressions from the original, and prepared the stone for the lithographic press with as many transfers of the original as they chose to print at one time. Other trades involved were proofers, layout men, pressmen (who printed the final process), the driers, cutters, and the die press operators. Trays were also handled by men in the assembly and packing departments.

Materials used in the manufacture were brushes, pallet knives, scrapers, ink, acid, paper, rollers, stick-ups needles. Most of these tools are not to be found in today's production of trays as mechanization and modernization have also brought about their change.

The decline of the tray manufacturing business (particularly beer trays) was plainly due to state laws being passed stating beer trays could not be used for advertising purposes; however, there are a few states that still allow this type of advertising.

Beer trays, or other advertising trays, which have been manufactured since **1950** have been made by American Can or Continental Can Companies. There is a

Vienna art plate. Tin 1907 calendar plate with pretty girl insert.
Harvard Brewing Company, Lowell, MA
Brewery: 1898 – 1918, 1933 – 1956

firm in Canada reproducing older Coca-Cola trays. They are made on highly mechanized equipment, and somehow in comparison, lack the feeling and charm of the older trays. Now that manufacturing competition is diminished, trays are no longer marked with the lithograph company.

How to Tell the Age of Advertising

In the past, a collector has had to resort to guess work, such as: the type of scene portrayed, period of clothing worn, and the type and location of the scene depicted. The following should be a valuable aid in determining age.

The Tuscarora Advertising Company the and Standard Advertising Company manufactured metal art ware items (trays & signs) from **1887** to **1901**. There is little doubt that they manufactured several of the earliest Coca-Cola trays (pre-**1904**), and many of the early beer and mineral water trays. Any tray in your collection marked with either of these two lithographers is undoubtedly **1901** or before. There were numerous breweries among their accounts, some of which were: Buffalo Brewing Company, Sacramento; The National Brewing Company, San Francisco; Anheuser-Busch, St. Louis. They merged as the Meek & Beach Company in **1901**.

The Meek and Beach Company's name appears on trays for only a few years. The exact dates are sketchy but **1901 – 1905** seems to be the most accurate. The Meek and Beach Company ceased to exist when Mr. Beach sold his interest in the company to Mr. Meek. Meek promptly renamed it the Tuscarora Company. With a change in "humility," a few months later, he modified it to the Meek Company. Two breweries having trays manufactured by Meek & Beach were: Harvard Brewing, Lowell, Massachusetts; Chartier's Valley Brewing Company, Carnegie, Pennsylvania.

The Meek Company came into existence after Mr. Beach sold his interests to Mr. Meek. The trays marked The Meek Company date from **1901** to **1909**. (You may find a Meek Company tray dated **1910**.) The following breweries had Meek manufacture trays for them: Rheingold Beer, New York; Olean Brewing Company, New York; Fred Sebring Brewing Company, Joliet, Illinois.

Oval tray. Cowboy on a horse.
National Beer, National Brewing
Company, San Francisco, CA
Slogan: The Best in the West
Tray manufactured by H.D. Beach
Company, 1901 – 1910
Brewery: 1884 – 1910
Size: 14" x 16"

*Circular tray. Classical image of
Indian princess in full costume.
Wieland's Extra Pale Lager
Kaufman & Strauss Lithograph Company
Brewery: 1900 – 1910
Size: 13"*

The Meek Company's name ceased to be put on trays in 1909 when they changed their name to the American Art Works.

The H.D. Beach Company dates from 1901 and has been in continuous business ever since. Some of the early beer trays are marked H.D. Beach Company, and date from 1901 to 1919. They did produce a few beer trays after prohibition, and they also manufactured mineral water and soda water trays after that date. The earliest Coca-Cola tray the Beach Company made is dated 1904, the very beautiful St. Louis Fair tray. The Buffalo Brewing Company tray (front cover) is marked by Beach, but in an unusual way. It says "Beach Art Display," and evidently was never made to be used as a tray, although collectors refer to it as such. The Lemp Brewing Company (now called Falstaff) also had several trays made by Beach with the same mark. Some of these trays are an outstanding 24" in diameter.

Additionally trays manufactured by the Beach Company at one time include: Harvard Brewing, Lowell; National Brewing, San Francisco; Union Brewing, Detroit; John Wieland, San Francisco; Ruhstaller's Brewing, Sacramento. (None of the H.D. Beach trays in my collection are date marked.)

Any tray marked with American Art Works is post-1908. The company was actually incorporated according to the corporate papers: "Whereas, at a meeting of the Directors of this company, held at the office of the company in Coshocton, Ohio, on the 30th day of November 1909, the following resolution was adopted: 'Resolved that this Board of Directors deem it advisable to change the name of this company from the Meek Company to the American Art Works and that the Articles of Incorporation be amended to change said name." The company continued in business and manufactured trays, signs, and other novelty items until 1950, when they ceased all operations. The buildings were only recently torn down.

American Art Works appears on many, many Coca-Cola trays dating from 1909. In fact, the 1909 tray is the first Coca-Cola tray bearing the lithograph mark of American Art Works. The earliest tray in my collection so marked is the tip tray, "Old Reliable Coffee." The mark says, "Copyright, 1907, The American Art Works, Successors to the Meek Company, Coshocton, Ohio." Although The

American Art Works did not incorporate until **1909**, they did put the copyright date of the picture on the tray, indicating that tray was manufactured in **1909**. American Art Works merely gave credit to the date the picture was first done by the artist. If a date does not appear on an American Art Works tray, and it is a beer tray, you may be certain it is pre-**1919**. They continued to make soft drink trays as well as other trays, dating from after **1919** through the '20s, '30s, and '40s. As many of you know, they manufactured at least one (often three different) Coca-Cola trays every year from **1922** to **1950**.

Breweries having trays made for them by American Art Works include: El Dorado Brewing, Stockton; Golden West Brewing, Oakland, California; Hagerstown Brewing, Hagerstown; Buffalo Brewing, Sacramento.

Bachrach Company (**1895 – 1917**) was a turn-of-the-century lithographing company, once located in San Francisco, but no longer in existence. All of their beer and mineral water trays should pre-date **1918**. Four trays in my collection with their mark are: John Wieland, San Francisco; Enterprise Brewing, San Francisco; Rainier Beer (Seattle Brewing & Malting), Seattle; Wunder Brewing, San Francisco.

Schonk & Company (**1890 – 1935?**) was located in Chicago, Illinois. All beer trays manufactured by them should pre-date **1919**. My research indicates they continued in business through at least **1935**, but if they manufactured beer trays from **1932** to **1935** I am not aware of them. Breweries that had trays made by Schonk & Company are: Jersey Creme, New Jersey; Columbia Brewing, Tacoma; Olympia Brewing, Tumwater; Terre Haute Brewing Company, Terre Haute.

Schonk & Company also manufactured trays for soft drink and mineral water companies. I have two Red Raven trays by them, and there's reason to believe they manufactured the larger 24" diameter tray (art display) of the same name.

Kaufmann & Strauss (**1890 – 1971?**) was located in New York City. At one time, it was probably the largest manufacturer of trays in the world. Most trays were marked Kaufmann & Strauss. They also manufactured thousands of metal signs and other novelties, advertising

Circular tray. Innocent looking Victorian lady.
"Evelyn Nesbitt," a girl in pink and white hooded coat.
Rainier Beer, Seattle Brewing &
Malting Company
Bachrach 1903
Brewery: 1892 – 1904, 1904 – 1906, 1906 – 1915
Size: 13½"

extensively all over the United States. *The Western Brewer's Handbook* of 1916 features one of their ads. They, or members of their family, may still be in business. A recent listing in the New York City phone directory revealed a Kaufmann & Company, Lithographer.

All of their trays, unless otherwise dated, are pre-1919. Breweries using Kaufmann & Strauss trays included: Akron Brewing Company, Akron; Los Angeles Brewing Company, Los Angeles; Ruhstaller's Brewing Company, Sacramento, and hundreds of others.

The American Can Company (1901 – present) is the largest manufacturer of tin lithographed items in the world today. They did make some early beer trays, and an example in my collection is an Anheuser-Busch tray dated 1914, showing a Mississippi River levee scene.

It is my conjecture that this company was primarily in the tin can production business and did not manufacture an abundance of trays. Many of the beautiful early 1900 tobacco tins were done by them.

The American Colortype Company (1930 –?) was incorporated by the American Art Works in 1930. The fact that it was located in Newark, and the fact that the American Art Works held their annual board meeting in the same city, may account for the consolidation. This company ordered thousands of trays from the American Art Works from 1930 to 1950. Christian Feigenspan Brewing Company (P.O.N. – Pride of Newark) ordered a large number of trays from American Colortype Company. There are countless other breweries and soft drink companies numbering among their accounts. I don't believe they manufactured beer trays prior to 1930. If this were true, all of their trays post-date 1929.

The Canadian-American Art Works, Limited, was initially organized as the Canadian Art Works on 3 January 1912. They were located in Montreal, Canada.

On February 1, 1912, Mr. C.R. Frederickson was appointed president. (Mr. Frederickson was also president of the American Art Works), and on December 2, 1913, the name was formally changed to the Canadian-American Art Works, Ltd. They continued in business until October 1946, manufacturing beer trays and signs for Canadian breweries.

"A Winner"

Opposite page: 1917 calendar.
Indian in a canoe with his kill.
Tadellos, Ruehl Brewing Company,
Chicago, IL
Slogan: Dark Export TADELLOS BEER
Malt Narra
Brewery: 1915 – 1925
Size: 15" x 20"

Above: Circular tray. Cowgirl with horse.
Yosemite Beer, Enterprise Brewing Company
San Francisco, CA
Brewery: 1892 – 1914, 1914 – 1920
Size: 12"

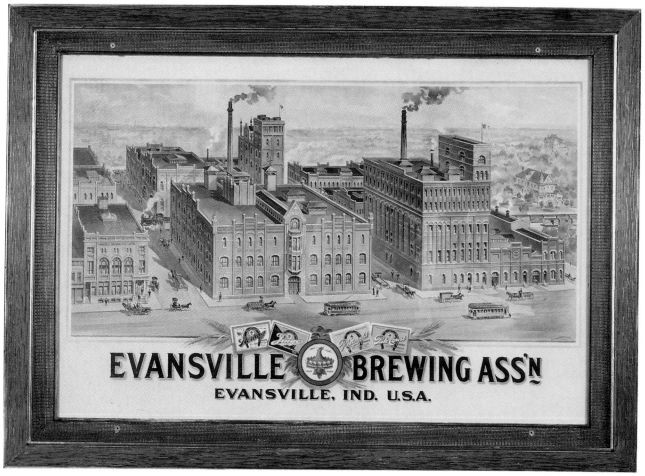

Brewery Company Art

In the late **1800**s and early **1900**s brewers distributed signs featuring their breweries to the taverns that served their products. This form of advertising is being used at the present time by some of our breweries.

These signs or lithos were usually paper, tin, cardboard, canvas, or in some cases, produced on wood.

The main brewery building was shown and on some examples other buildings were pictured, such as the bottling house, warehouse, ice house, stables and the brewer's home. The brewers' portraits were inserted on some of these scenes, making them even more interesting and valuable.

These scenes displayed the American Flag flying above the brewery and black smoke belching from the smokestacks — probably representing signs of patriotism and good economy.

Opposite page, top: Brewery poster.
The Eberhardt & Ober Brewing Company,
Allegheny, PA
Brewery: 1883 – 1899
Size: 44" x 28"

Opposite page, bottom: Brewery poster,
manufacturing facility.
Evansville Brewing Association,
Evansville, IN
Brewery: 1894 – 1915
Size: 36" x 24"

Below: Manufacture poster Betz Brewery.
Ale, Porter & Lager Beer
John F. Betz & Son
Brewery: 1880 – 1889
Size: 32" x 22"

At right: The H. Fischer Brewery, Hartford, CT

Below, left: Printed cardboard poster.
John L. Sullivan - Champion Pugilist of the World
Bavarian's Old Style
Bavarian Brewing, Covington, KY
Slogan: Bavarian's Old Style, "A Man's Beer"
Brewery: 1898 – 1913, 1933, 1959
Size: 17" x 24"

Below, right: Fox Deluxe statue.
Peter Fox Brewing Company, Chicago, IL
Slogan: Don't say Fox, Say Fox Deluxe
Brewery: 1933 – 1955
Size: 16"

Opposite page:
Tin over cardboard sign.
John L. Sullivan - Super Champion. Fighter
in stance.
Hohenadel Beer. John Hohenadel Brewery, Inc.,
Philadelphia, PA
Slogan: Well Earned Supremacy
Brewery: 1935 – 1953
Size: 17" x 23"

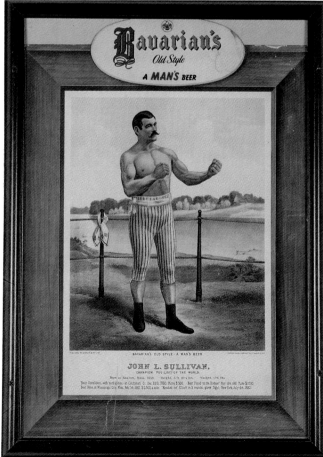

Printed four-color lithograph of manufacturing facility plus inset of Mr. Centlivre.
Lager Beer Brewed in Wood and Glass, C.L. Centlivre Brewing Company, Inc.,
Fort Wayne, IN
Slogan: Brewers and Bottlers of Lager Beer
Brewery: 1893 – 1918
Size: 36" x 24"

C.L. Centlivre Brewing Company
In 1862 Charles Centlivre settled in Fort Wayne, where he was joined by his father and brother, Frank. They had been coopers in Louisville, Ohio, and later brewers in McGregor, Iowa. With their own hands, they built a primitive brewhouse on land now occupied by this brewery. That brewery developed into this plant. A bottling department was established in 1876, a new brewhouse was erected in 1902.

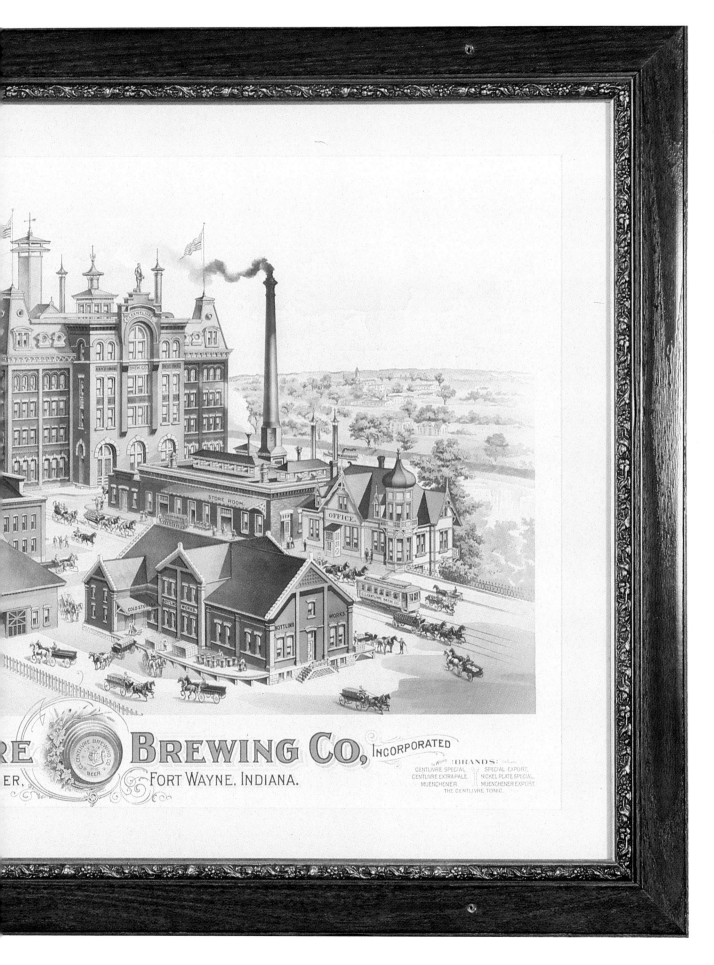

RE BREWING CO., INCORPORATED

ER, FORT WAYNE, INDIANA.

BRANDS:
CENTLIVRE SPECIAL, SPECIAL EXPORT,
CENTLIVRE EXTRAPALE, NICKEL PLATE SPECIAL,
MUENCHENER, MUENCHENER EXPORT,
THE CENTLIVRE TONIC.

Self-framed tin sign of factory scene. Chattanooga
Brewing Company, Chattanooga, TN
Slogan: The South's Model Brewery
Brewery: 1890 – 1915
Size: 22" x 30"

Chattanooga Brewing Company
   In 1888 Conrad Geise and E.D. Kohn erected
a brewery at Chattanooga which was the start
of the plant that was purchased in 1890 and
became the Chattanooga Brewing Company. In
1891 – 92 a new brew-house, seven stories high,
was built, a mechanical refrigerating plant was
installed, the storage cellars were enlarged, and
other improvements were made. The total cost
of this project was $200,000.

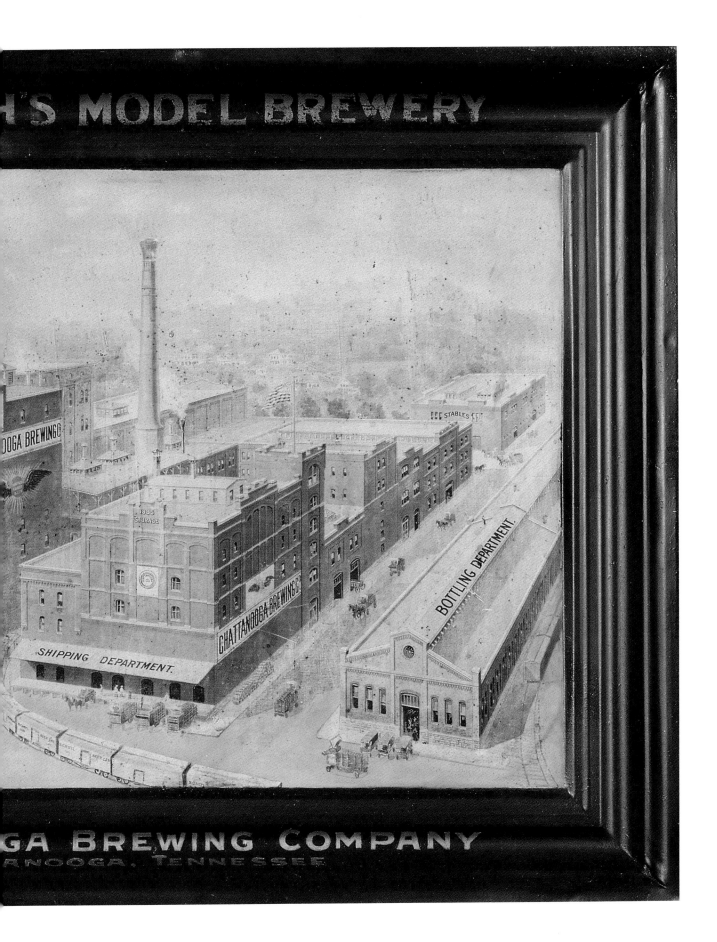

35

Litho sign of brewery. Litho by Gugler, Milwaukee, WI
XX Pale & Standard Muenchner, Born & Company,
Brewers & Bottlers of Capital Brands,Columbus, OH
Brewery: 1870 – 1904
Size: 38" x 27"

Born & Company

This brewing company had its origin in a small brewery founded by Conrad Born Sr., in 1859. It established a bottling department in the late 1860s or 1870s. By 1903 they were bottling about 25,000 barrels of beer from their annual capacity of 100,000 barrels. Refrigeration machinery was installed in 1889. Malt had been made at the plant since it was founded.

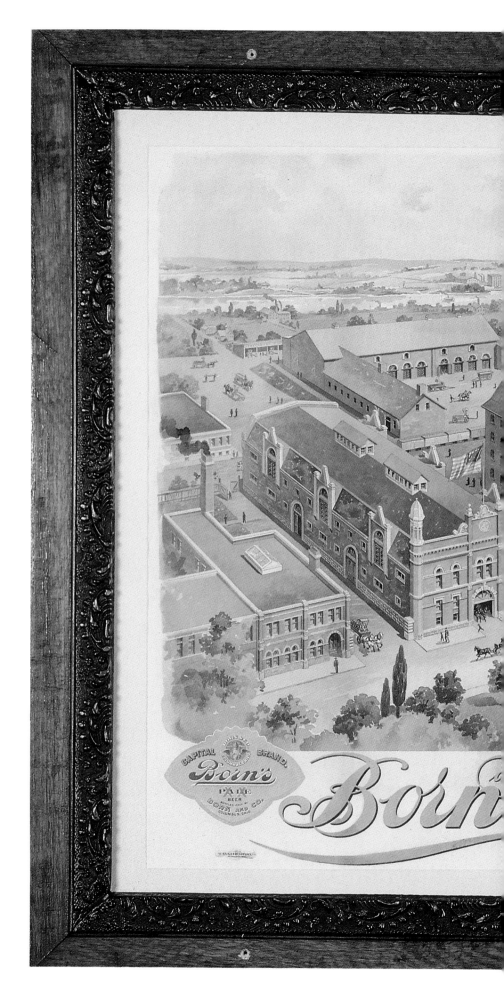

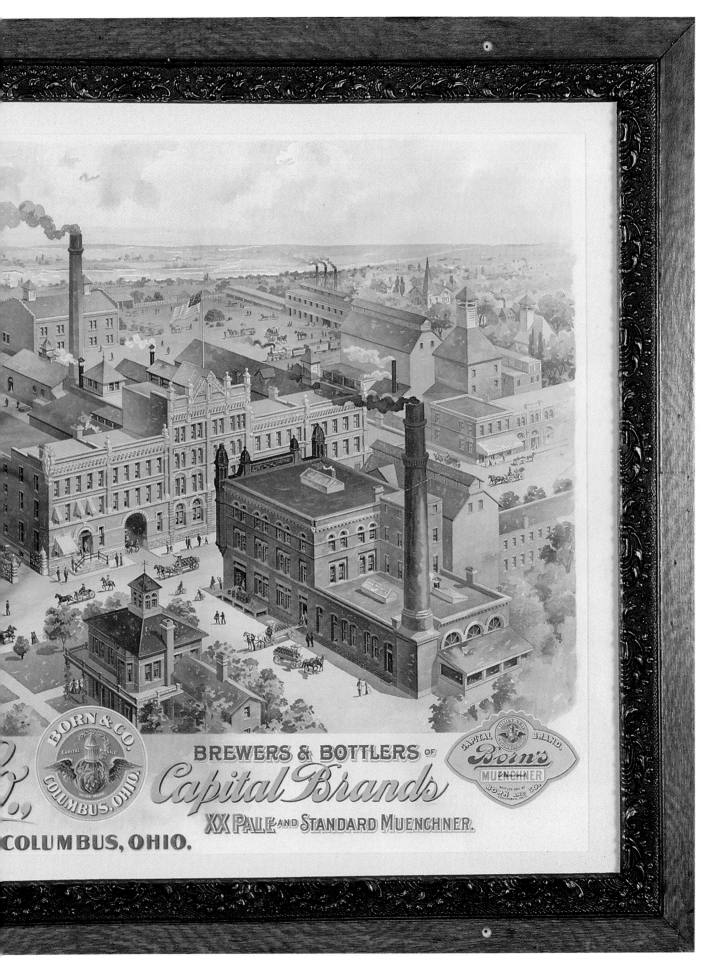

BORN & CO.
CAPITAL BRAND
COLUMBUS, OHIO.

BREWERS & BOTTLERS OF

Capital Brands

XX PALE AND STANDARD MUENCHNER.

COLUMBUS, OHIO.

CAPITAL BRAND.
Born's
MUENCHNER
BORN AND CO.
COLUMBUS, OHIO.

At right: Paper litho sign. Elves working, eating, and drinking in the brewery.
Elfenbrau. C. & J. Michel Brewing Company, LaCrosse, WI
Slogan: Elfenbrau - Wholesome as Sunshine
Brewery: 1882 – 1920
Size: 23½" x 26"

Bottom: Plaster statue of brewery elf with bottle.
Elfenbrau, C. & J. Michel Brewing Company, LaCrosse, WI
Slogan: Wholesome as Sunshine
Brewery: 1882 – 1920
Size: 20"

C. & J. Michel Brewing Company
The brewery was founded by C. & J. Michel in 1857. They made about 1,000 barrels of lager beer during their first year oj brewing.

At left: Brewery scene sign.
Nude sitting on top of world and manufacturing plant.
Schlitz, Joseph Schlitz Brewing Company,
Milwaukee, WI
Brewery: 1874 – 1920, 1933 – 1981
Size: 38" x 26"

Below: Plaster molded sign.
Stegmaier, arm holding a beer.
Stegmaier, Wilkes-Barre, PA
Brewery: 1897 – 1920, 1933 – 1974
Size: 25½" x 31"

Self-framed tin.
Export Beer, Gold Seal.
Two bottles featured with brewery.
Export Beer, First National Brewing Company, McKeesport, PA
Slogan: We Use Water From This Historical Indian Spring For All Our Beer
Brewery: 1901 – 1904, 1904 – 1920
Size: 28" x 36"

First National Brewing Company
This brewery was organized in 1901 and its first brew was marketed on May 1, 1902. They commenced bottling in August.

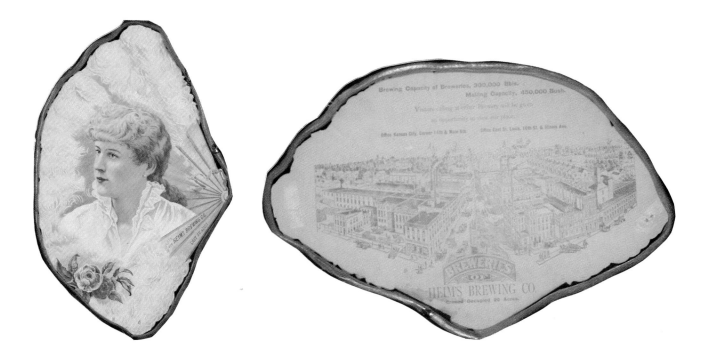

Above, left, and right: Sign. Victorian
lady on a cardboard shaped fan.
Brewery scene on back.
Heim's Brewing Company, 10 Street
& Illinois Ave., East St. Louis, IL
Brewery: 1880 – 1889
Size: 10" x 15"

At right: Paper litho sign.
H. Clausen & Son Brewers, New York,
NY
Brewery: 1866 – 1888
Size: 16½" x 23½"

Opposite page: Printed paper sign.
Pilsener Private Stock Export. Lion
on top of world with bottle of beer.
The Kamm & Schellinger Brewing
Company, Mishawaka, IN
Slogan: Challenge The World
Litho by Gugler, Milwaukee, WI.
Brewery: 1887 – 1918
Size: 22" x 33½"

Paper sign of brewery surrounded by scenes of workers in brewery.
Export Beer, Walter Brothers Brewing, Island Brewery, Menasha, WI
Brewery: 1891 – 1920, 1933 – 1956
Size: 36" x 28"

Walter Brothers Brewing Company
In 1888 the brewery was purchased by Walter Brothers & Fries. It became the Walter Brothers Brewing Company in 1893, with Charles Walter as president. The malthouse was built in 1891. In 1894 – 95 the stock house was remodeled and new cellars added, the capacity of the plant being enlarged to a 125 barrel outfit.

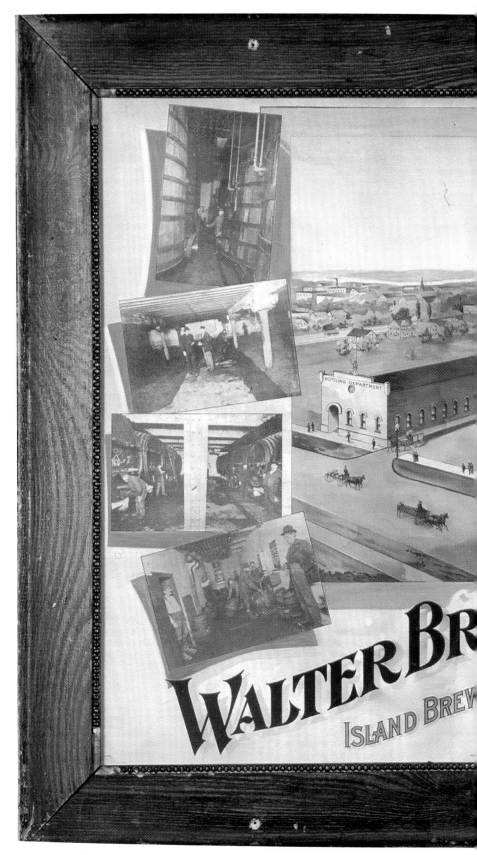

BREWING CO.
MENASHA, WIS.

It's spring and Bock Beer is on tap! These gentlemen dressed in their spring attire are about to taste the new brew. (The frowns should turn to smiles.)

Bock advertising, such as the Rainier sign above the bar, were usually so colorful and clever they caught the customers' attention. They served their purposes!

48

Legend of Bock Beer

"Since the Middle Ages, the first harbinger of spring has been the tapping of kegs filled with dark, creamy Bock Beer.

The exact time of its arrival varies in different locales, but the posting of 'the sign of the goat,' whatever the day, is a better sign of spring than the coming of the first robin.

How the 'goat' came to symbolize Bock Beer is told in many ways. A favorite is that in the town of Einbock, Germany, famous for the potency of its dark Beer Two stalwarts held a contest of beer-drinking prowess. One of the contestants fell from a barrel he was straddling and rolled over to where a goat was standing. He vowed it was not the beer that had toppled him, but that 'Der Bock' has

butted him. Since bock in German means goat, and the town of Einbock is pronounced Ein*bock*; it is likely that both the name Bock and the sign of the goat, to designate the dark beer, came about in the manner related.

The distinctive flavor and dark color of Bock Beer is due to the special malt used in its brewing. The malt for Bock Beer is roasted or carmelized, and the beer itself is aged longer than lighter beers.

You'll find that the dark creamy goodness of Pabst Bock Beer is refreshment to give you a bright cheerful and spring-like outlook on life. Shortly after 1844, Pabst — America's Oldest National Brewer — began to brew its rich, ruby-brown Bock. It's been brewing fine Bock, in accord with the ancient tradition ever since."

Above: Paper sign. Otto Vill, Proprietor.
Minnesota City Brewery, Minnesota City, MN
Brewery: 1869 – 1915
Size: 24" x 30"

ESTABLISHED 1872

Chicago Engraving Co.

ARTISTS·ENGRAVERS ❦❦
& COLOR PLATE MAKERS
350-352 WABASH AVE.
CHICAGO,
PHONE·HAR·623

Gentlemen-
        Did you receive our recent letter relative
to Bock Beer Signs for 1907 delivery?

        We fear that you didn't as our proposition
is so very liberal that you surely would have responded
before now.

        You know as well as we do that such attrac-
tive hangers have never been offered you before at
similar prices.   Another thing, they are not old
fashioned subjects that have been displayed on every
corner for the past ten or twenty years, on the contrary, each one is entirely original, made up along
modern lines and bound to command attention wherever
you put them.

        The bold lettering which we put on each
sign enables the passer-by to read it readily, the
colors are bright and flashy -- and broadly speaking,
these hangers are perfectly made in every respect.

        Now, don't wait until the last moment to
place your order, as to make prompt delivery it is
quite necessary that we hear from you just as soon
as possible.   We hereby quote the following prices
for immediate acceptance,--
  200 Complete hangers, tinned top and bottom,$ 19.00
  300 Complete hangers, tinned top and bottom, 27.00
  500 Complete hangers, tinned top and bottom, 42.50
 1000 Complete hangers, tinned top and bottom, 80.00
 2000 Complete hangers, tinned top and bottom, 140.00

        If you want to boom your Bock Beer sales
next season simply display our signs about town,
they'll get the business all right.   Try them.

                    Very truly yours,
                    CHICAGO ENGRAVING COMPANY.

                    Dept. of Modern Publicity,

                    By

Dict.F.M.S.Jr.-F.
#2   Manager.

Above: Chicago Engraving Co, 1907 letter quoting prices for ordering
Bock Beer signs — don't bother to reorder, prices have changed!

Top: Die cut, Mother passing out Christmas ornaments to daughter by the Christmas tree.
Moerschel Brewing Company, Sedalia, MO
Brewery: 1897 – 1919
Size: 15" x 21"

Bottom: Trade card.
Falstaff & Lemp, Wm. J. Lemp
Brewing Company, St. Louis, MO
Brewery: 1892 – 1919
Size: 10" x 4¾"

Top: Die cut, 3-D shadow box.
Goats pulling beautiful carriage with
lovely lady passengers.
Golden Grain Belt, Minneapolis
Brewing Company, Minneapolis, MN
Brewery: 1893 – 1920, 1933 – 1967
Size: 14" x 9"

Bottom: Self-framed tin sign of
picnic on a hill overlooking brewery.
Schmulbach Brewing Company,
Wheeling, WV
Brewery: 1882 – 1914
Size: 33" x 23"

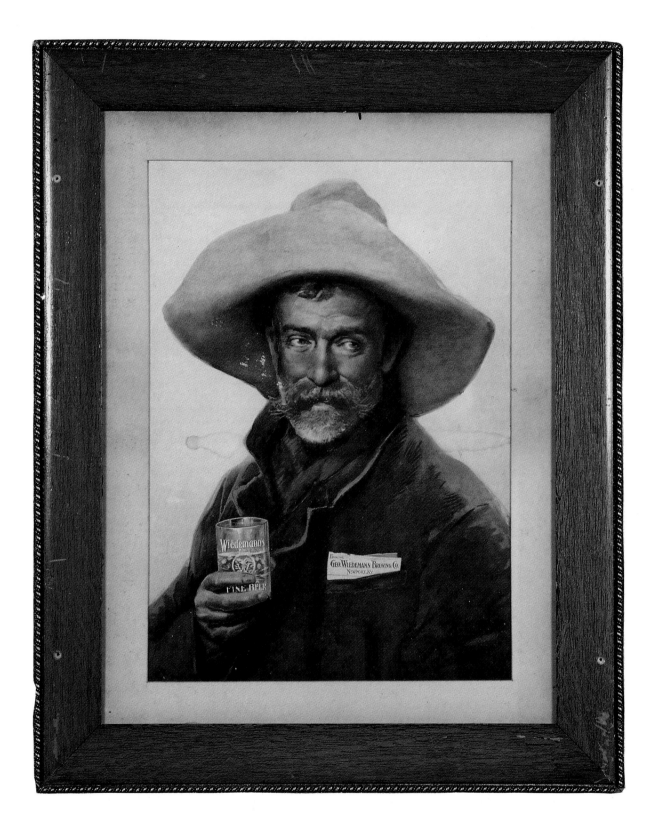

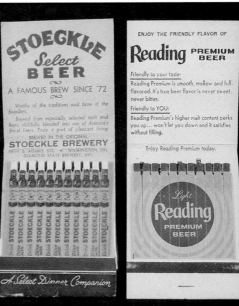

Top, left: Novelty item, pack of cigarettes.
The Burkhardt Brewing Company, Akron, OH
Brewery: 1933 – 1956
Size: 2⅛" x 2¾"

Top, right: Novelty items, large match books. Stoeckle Brewery and Diamond State Brewery, Inc., Wilmington, DE
Brewery: 1902 – 1920, 1936 – 1954
Size: 3½" x 8"

The Old Reading Brewery, Inc.,
Reading, PA
Brewery: 1933 – 1965
Size: 3½" x 8"

Opposite page: Paper litho sign. Oakwood frame. Gold prospector with etched glass of Wiedemann's Beer. Note: White bill of sale in jacket pocket says George Wiedemann Brewing Company, Newport, Ky. Glass is etched with Wiedemann's FINE BEER.
Wiedemann's Fine Beer, Geo. Wiedemann Brewing Company, Newport, KY
Brewery: 1890 – 1918
Size: 16" x 22"

Bottom photo: Oakwood wooden sign. Royal flush of clubs.
The Geo. Wiedemann Brewing Company, Newport, KY
Brewery: 1936 – 1967
Size: 14" x 20"

56

56

Brewery Signs

The porcelain sign was developed in the **1880s**, probably in Europe. Many early porcelain signs advertising American companies were produced in England. At least a few were produced in Germany. Porcelain signs do not have the detail of lithographed paper or tin, and the color is not quite as brilliant as reverse glass. The end result of the porcelain process is glass on steel. It is very durable and the bright colors resist fading.

Corner signs were usually made of enamel, tin, milk glass, or vitriol. Corner signs were made to fit on the corners of buildings and were made of enamel and tin. The glass signs were displayed in the bar areas.

Opposite page: Self-framed tin sign. Four bottles of beer, cigar and mug on table. New Brew and Bohemia, Buffalo Brewing Company, Sacramento, CA Brewery: 1890 – 1897, 1934 – 1942 Size: 22" x 28"

Below: Rectangle metal sign, double sided with name, Edelweiss Beer Size: 18" x 12"

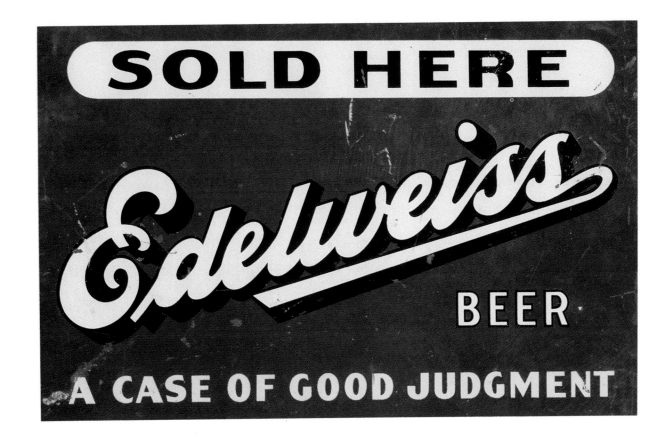

*Top: Mug. Neillsville Brewery,
Neillsville, WI
Slogan: King of Beer
Brewery: 1898 – 1920*

*Bottom: Oval tray. Picture of
King Gambrinus, King of Beer.
Gambrinus Pale Beer, August Wagner
& Sons Brewing Company,
Columbus, OH
Slogan: The Beer Your Daddy Drank
Brewery: 1933 – 1937
H.D. Beach Co., Coshocton, OH
Size: 12½" x 15"*

*Opposite page: King Gambrinus
pictured on the Gambrinus Brewery
Building in Columbus, OH.*

Gambrinus
Father or King of Real Beer

There are many mythical tales which, variously colored by different nations, are current concerning the father of real beer. We say real beer, for, although the use of a wine-like beverage extracted from barley extends far into the pre-historic ages, real beer (that is, the drink known to us by that name) is of more recent origin; yet, as to place and date of the latter, nothing definite can be known. While some attribute the invention of hopped malt-beer to Jan Primus, a scion of the stock of Burgundy princes, who lived about the year 1251, others ascribe it to Jean Sans Pear (1371 – 1419), otherwise known as Ganbrivius. A corruption of either name may plausibly be shown to have resulted in the present name of the King of Beer, Gambrinus, whom we are accustomed to see represented in the habit of a knight of the Middle Ages, with the occasional addition of a crown. Popular imagination, it seems, attached such great importance to beer that in according the honor of its invention, it could not be satisfied with anything less than a king.

Right: Old King paper beer label.
Southwestern Brewing Corp., Oklahoma City, OK
Slogan: The Quality Beer

Below: Paper sign. Brewery with King Gambrinus insert.
W&L Sebald, Middletown Brewery, Middletown, OH
Brewery: 1864 – 1886, 1886 – 1919
Size: 29" x 22"

Opposite page: Porcelain corner sign.
King Gambrinus sitting on throne.
The Gambrinus Brewing Co., Columbus, OH
Slogan: Quality Beer
Brewery: 1906 – 1919
Size: 16" x 24"

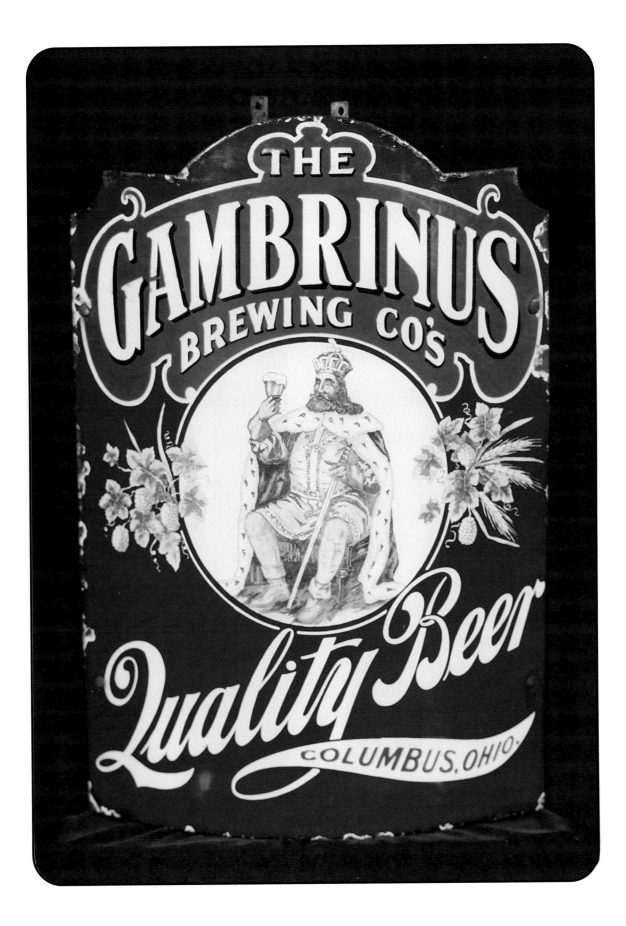

Tin sign, embossed. Thanks for repealing prohibition.
Fort Pitt Beer, Pittsburgh, PA
Slogan: Thanks To Our Courageous President and
sound thinking members of Congress and US Senators
for this delicious Fort Pitt Beer
Brewery: 1933 – 1955
Size: 24" x 21"

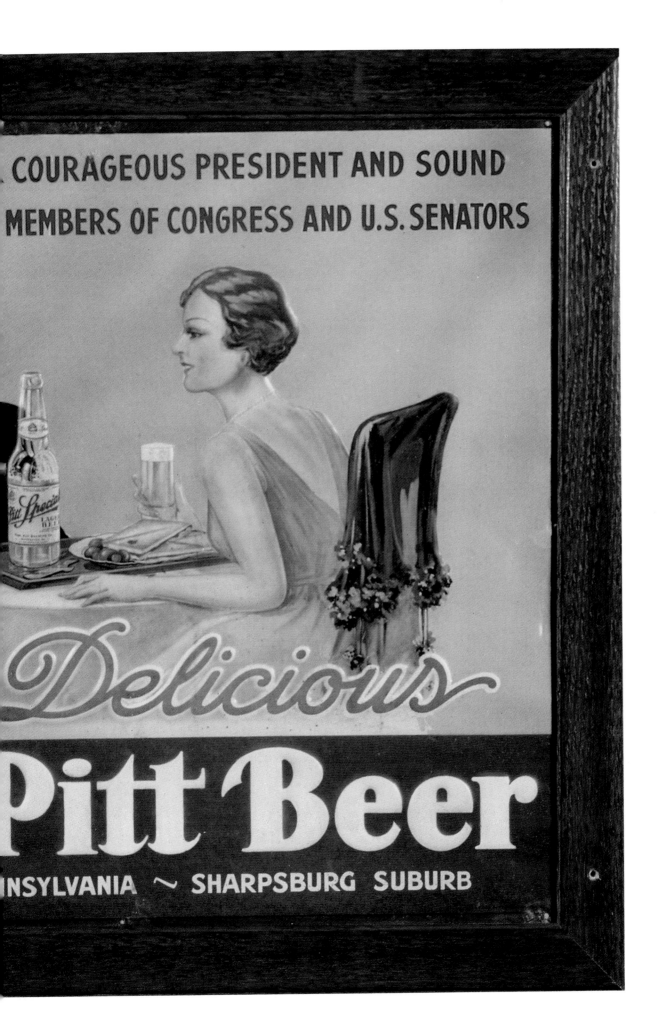

Top: Porcelain sign, name and logo.
Gold Label Beer, Walter Brothers
Brewing Company, Menasha, WI
Slogan: It's in the Brewing
Brewery: 1891 – 1920, 1933 – 1956
Size: 17"

Bottom: Porcelain sign, #9 Horlacher's
Beer.
Slogan: 9 Months Old Bottle Beer
Brewery: 1902 – 1921, 1933 – 1978
Size: 18"

Opposite page: Curved porcelain
corner sign, company logo.
Hochgreve Beer, Hochgreve Brewing
Company, Green Bay, WI
Brewery: 1894 – 1920, 1933 – 1949
Size 14" x 20"

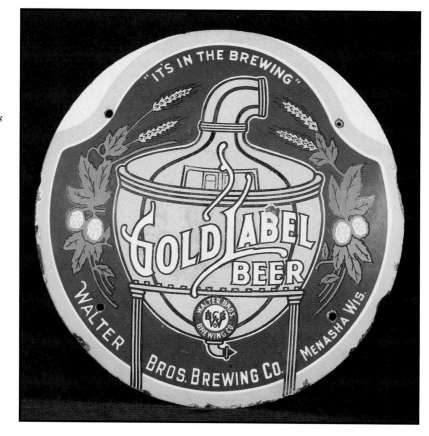

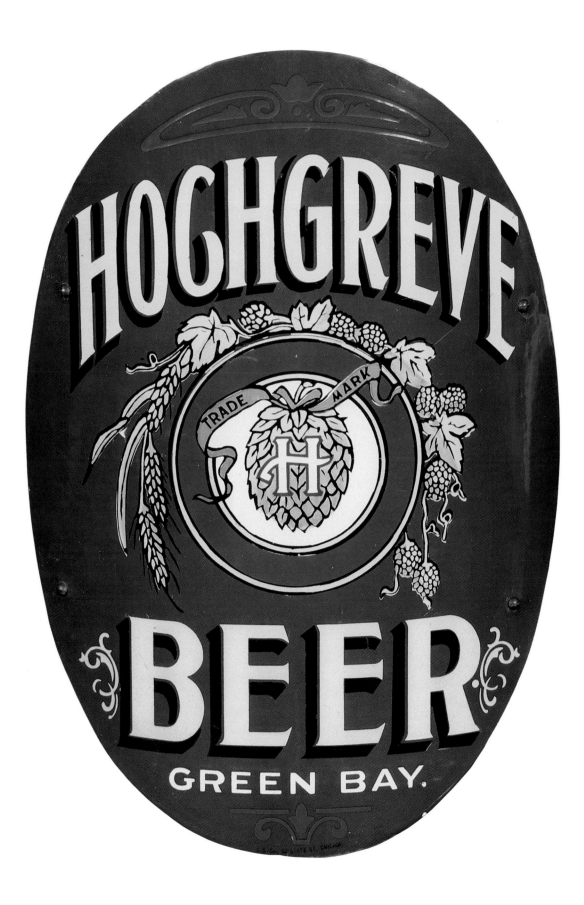

THE HOSTER-COLUMBUS ASSOCIATED BREWERIES CO.
COLUMBUS, OHIO. U.S.A.

66

Opposite page: Self-framed tin sign. Turkey with beer.
Famous Beer, The Hoster-Columbus Associated Breweries Company, Columbus, OH
Brewery: 1904 – 1919
Size: 22" x 28"

Top: Metal flange sign, painted on both sides.
Age-Dated Beer
Lucky Lager Brewing Company
Brewery: 1950 – 1964
Size: 12" x 15"

Bottom: Self-framed tin sign. Two gentlemen blowing a flute and clarinet. Note: Calendar on wall April 7, 1933, in red (Day Prohibition ended).
Hudepohl Beer, Hudepohl Brewing Company, Cincinnati, OH
Slogan: Something To Blow About
Brewery: 1934 – 1986
Size: 19¼" x 15½"

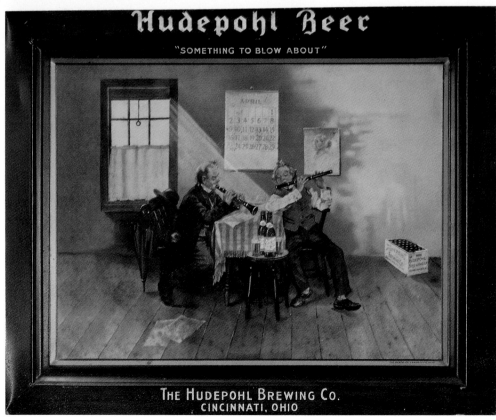

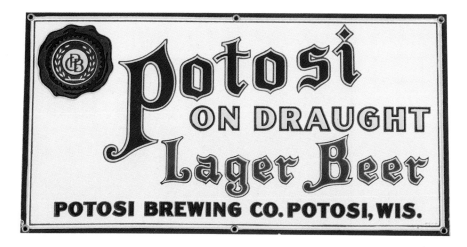

Opposite page: Tin sign with rolled corners.
Buergerliches Brauhaus, Leitmeritz Boehmen.
Imported Pilsner, R. Naegeli's Sons, Hoboken, NJ
Size: 17" x 20½"

Top: Porcelain sign.
Potosi On Draft Lager Beer,
Potosi Brewing Company, Potosi, WI
Brewery: 1933 – 1972
Size: 20½" x 11"

Center: Curved porcelain corner sign.
Princeton Tiger Brew, Princeton, WI
Slogan: The Beer with a Purr
Brewery: 1866 Established.
Size: 14" x 20"

Bottom: Tin over cardboard.
Joseph Schlitz Brewing Company,
Milwaukee, WI
Slogan: Bless her heart!
Brewery: 1858 – 1920, 1933 – 1981
Size: 24" x 12"

Tin sign.
L. Schlather Brewing Company,
Cleveland, OH
Brewery: 1884 – 1902
Size: 36" x 24"

L. Schlather Brewing Company
The brewery was established in 1857 by L. Schlather upon the site of this plant. In 1884 it became the L. Schlather Brewing Company, its sales were 50,000 barrels that year. In 1902 the brewery was purchased by the Cleveland and Sandusky Brewing Company.

STABLES

CLEVELAND, O.

Top: Curved porcelain corner sign.
George Walter's Adler Bräu
Appleton Beer, Geo. Walter Brewing
Company, Appleton, WI
Size: 14" x 20"

Bottom: Oval tray.
Gold Label Beer, Walter Bros. Brew-
ing Company, Menasha, WI
Slogan: Brewed From Selected Malt
Best Imported Hops
Copyright: H.D. Beach Co.
Brewery: 1888 – 1920, 1933 – 1956
Size: 16½" x 13½"

Self-framed tin sign. U.S. Cavalry soldier drinking beer.
Joseph Schlitz Brewing Company, Milwaukee, WI
Slogan: Hits The Mark
Schlitz The Beer That Made Milwaukee Famous
Brewery: 1858 – 1920, 1933 – 1981
Size: 9½" x 22"

Below: Metal flange, double sided sign.
Joseph Schlitz Brewing Company,
Milwaukee, WI
Slogan: Schlitz The Beer That Made
Milwaukee Famous
Brewery: 1858 – 1920, 1933 – 1981
Size: 23" x 19½"

Opposite page: Porcelain sign.
Stegmaier Beer, Stegmaier Brewing
Company, Wilkes-Barre, PA
Brewery: 1880 – 1920, 1933 – 1974
Size: 14" x 25"

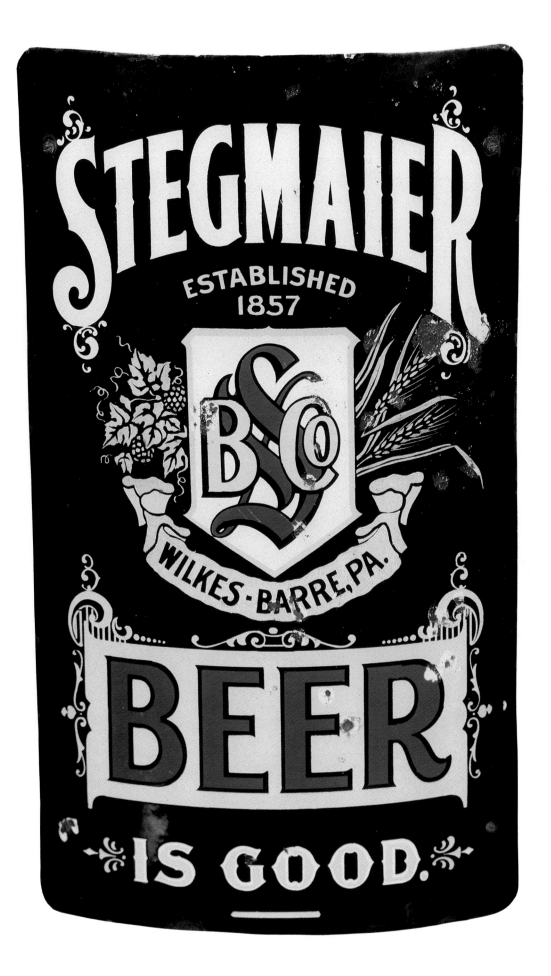

Brewery Trays

Trays are usually made of tin. There are exceptions, such as aluminum, brass, silver plated, and the latest, plastic. The multicolor lithographic designs on the trays were originated by the breweries, others were offered as "stock" illustrations by the tray manufacturers. Stock means the picture was standard and the ordering brewery simply specified copy which made tray purchasing more economical. There are four main themes central to tray design. The first of course, is pretty girls. Whether a tray is from **1909** or in the **1990s** an alluring pretty girl is very likely to be pictured. A second is the product a shot of a frothy glass, the bottle, or the can. The third is to show the brewery plant itself. The fourth, the mighty horse, which was well known by everyone.

Opposite page: Tin sign. Blatz, Blatz
Brewing Company, Milwaukee, WI
Copyright: Chas. W. Shonk, Chicago
Brewery: 1852 – 1920, 1933 – 1958
Size: 12"

Below: Tray. Cascade Beer, Union Brewing & Malting Company, San Francisco, CA
Slogan: We never disagree about the purity of the nation's favorite
Brewery: 1902 – 1916
Size: 10½" x 13¼"

Opposite page: Oval tray.
John A. Semrád & Bros., Brewers & Bottlers, Highland, WI
Slogan: Bottlers of the Famous Bohemian Export Beer
Copyright: Meek & Beach Coshocton
Brewery: 1893 – 1904
Size: 13½" x 16½"

Top: Oval tray with picture of owner, John Zynda.
Crystal Pale, John Zynda & Sons, Detroit, MI
Brewery: 1886 – 1919, 1933 – 1948
Size: 14" x 17"

John Zynda (1859 – 1927) immigrated to the United States from Poland in 1880 and founded the White Eagle Brewery in Detroit. In 1912 the name was changed to John Zynda & Sons. Mr. Zynda owned and operated the brewery from 1885 until his death in 1927, at which time his sons took over the business. The brewery survived through prohibition and lasted until 1948. This information was contributed by Mr. Zynda's great-grandson, Frank Zynda.

Bottom: Montage—Bottle & Tray
Hensler's Popular Beer. Brewed and bottled by Joseph Hensler Brewing Co., Newark, NJ
Slogan: Brewed Today Grandfather's Way
Light-Mild-Satisfying.
Brewery: 1933 – 1958
Tray size: 12"

Top: Circular tray.
Derby King Beer, Southern Breweries,
Inc., Norfolk, VA
Brewery: 1934 – 1942
Size: 13"

Bottom: Circular tray.
Dubuque Beer, Dubuque Brewing &
Malting Company, Dubuque, IA
Brewery: 1896 – 1916
Size: 12½"

Opposite page: Circular tray.
Dixie Beer Kentucky Pride,
Lexington Brewing Company,
Lexington, KY
Slogan: That Good Beer — The
Beer of Quality
Brewery: 1897 – 1918, 1934 – 1934
Size: 13"

DUESSELDORFER

"GRAND PRIZE WINNERS"

GRAND PRIZE, ST. LOUIS, 1904. GOLD MEDALS, PARIS 1900 AND BELGIUM 1905. GRAND PRIZE, GOLD MEDAL AND CROSS OF HONOR, FRANCE, 1906.

Circular sign. Duesseldorfer.
Slogan: Grand Prize Winners
Grand Prize — St. Louis 1904
Gold Medals — Paris 1900 and
Belgium 1905
Grand Prize, Gold Medal and
Cross of Honor, France, 1906
This tray emphasizes the healthful
attributes of beer
Size: 12"

Oval tray.
Excelsior Brewing Company,
Brooklyn, NY
Brewery: 1896 – 1932
Size: 16½" x 13½"

Opposite page: Oval self-framed tin sign
and actual bottle of Tonic in front of tray.
Fehr's Malt Tonic, Frank Fehr Brewing
Company, Louisville, KY
Slogan: For Health and Strength
Copyright: H.D. Beach Co.
Brewery: 1890 – 1918, 1933 – 1964
Size: 22½" x 28"

SELECT

HEMRICH BRO'S BREWING CO.

PORTER

LAGER BEER

SEATTLE, U.S.A.

EXPORT

Opposite page: Oval tray. Victorian lady. Porter-Select-Lager Beer-Export, Hemrich Brothers Brewing Company, Seattle, WA
Size: 13" x 16"

Top: Circular tray. Elf sitting on a keg of beer.
Gruenewald Beer, Gruenewald Brewery, Inc., Philadelphia, PA
 Brewery: 1934 – 1935
 Size: 13"

Bottom: Circular tray. "Mildred" Inland Pride, Inland Brewing & Malting Company, Spokane, WA
 Slogan: "Inland Pride" Queen of all bottled beer
 Copyright: The Meek Litho Co.
 Brewery: 1901 – 1915
 Size: 13"

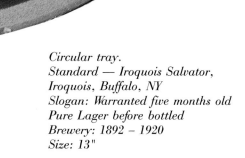

Circular tray.
Standard — Iroquois Salvator,
Iroquois, Buffalo, NY
Slogan: Warranted five months old
Pure Lager before bottled
Brewery: 1892 – 1920
Size: 13"

Circular tray.
Lackawanna Brewing Company, Scranton, PA
Copyright: Haeusermann Litho-NY-Chicago
Brewery: 1896 – 1897
Size: 13½"

Circular tray.
Lagers Ale & Porter,
Hanover Brewing Company, Danville, PA
Brewery: 1905 – 1915.
Chas. W. Shonk Litho Co., Chicago
Size: 12"

Circular tray. McAvoy's Malt, Marrow
McAvoy Brewery
Slogan: "NOT" Made In Germany
Brewery: 1887 – 1930
Size: 12"

Above: Circular tray.
Malt Wein, Dallas Brewery-Extract
Department, Dallas, TX
Slogan: Tickled Cus Mama Is
Going To Open The Bottle
Brewery: 1893 – 1901
Size: 13"

Opposite page, top: Oval tray.
Nonpareil Export.
The Foss-Schneider Brewing
Company, Cincinnati, OH
Brewery: 1884 – 1919
Size: 18½" x 15¼"

Opposite page, bottom: Oval tray.
Bohemian-Export-Bavarian-Dopplbrau-
Select-Blue Ribbon, Pabst, Milwaukee, WI
Slogan: Perfection and Purity Make
Pabst The Popular Beer
Copyright: Chas. W. Shonk Litho-Chicago
Brewery: 1880, 1920 – 1923
Size: 18½" x 15¼"

Top: Circular tray.
Pale Select Beer, Koppitz-Melchers Brewing Company, Detroit, MI
Slogan: The Drink of Every Season, Quality — The Reason
Copyright: Chas. W. Shonk
Brewery: 1891 – 1919
Size: 12"

Bottom: Montage. Two bottles never opened, with real blue ribbons on neck bands, two foam scrapers, Pabst Blue Ribbon on foam scrapers.
Pabst Blue Ribbon, Pabst Brewing Company.
Brewery: 1889 – 1920, 1938 – 1985, 1985 – present.

The Story of the Blue Ribbon

In 1882, the Ph. Best Brewing Company (later to become Pabst) began tying a blue ribbon around the neck of its Select brand of beer. This was an attempt to promote their bottled beer sales. Customers began to request "the bottle with the blue ribbon" and Select sales were on the rise. In 1892, Pabst was purchasing and tying, by hand, on the bottles more than 300,000 yards of blue silk ribbon a year. In 1895, the words Blue Ribbon were added to the label and in 1897 they replaced Select. In 1900, the Blue Ribbon name was registered.

CRYING FOR
Frank Fehr Brewing Co.'s
BEER.

*Left: Calendar. Stork with 12 babies of different
nationalities, each holding a calendar with a month of
the year.*
Pabst, Pabst Extract, Milwaukee, WI
Pabst Brewery Co.
Copyright: 1904
Brewery: 1889 – 1920, 1938 – present
Size: 10" x 27"

Top: Trade card.
Frank Fehr Brewing Co., Louisville, KY
Brewery: 1890 – 1918, 1933 – 1964
Size: 3¾" x 6½"

Oval tray. Beer, Ale & Porter,
The Home Brewing Company,
Shenandoah, PA
Brewery: 1899 – 1920
Artist: 1905, Chas. Ehler
Size: 13½" x 16½"

Oval tray. Prima Brew, Independent
Brewing Association, Chicago, IL
Brewery: 1890 – 1909, 1909 – 1920
Size: 13½" x 16½"

Circular tray. Hawaiian in an outrigger. Primo Beer, Honolulu Brewing & Malting Company, Ltd., Honolulu, HI
Brewery: 1900 – 1920
Size: 13"

Circular tray. Voigt's Rheingold Beer,
Voight's, Detroit, MI
Brewery: 1888 – 1919
Size: 12"

Top: Circular tray.
Maier Brewing Company,
Los Angeles, CA
Slogan: The Standard of Perfection
Brewery: 1882 – 1907, 1907 – 1920
Size: 13"

Bottom: Oval tray.
Pilsener Export, Grand Rapids Brewing Company, Grand Rapids, MI
Slogan: Silver Foam Our Special Brew
Brewery: 1893 – 1919
Size: 16" x 13"

Opposite page: Upright rectangle tray. Silver
Label, Antigo Brewing Company, Antigo, WI
Slogan: The Two Winners Silver Label
Brewery: 1895 – 1920
Size: 12" x 17"

Top: Tin sign, pennant shape.
Embossed bottle of beer on sign.
Sterling Super-Brew, Sterling Brewery, Inc.,
Evansville, IN
Brewery: 1933 – 1964, 1964 – 1968
Size: 9" top, 3" bottom, 17½" long

Bottom: Circular tray.
Sterling Beer, Evansville Brewing
Association, Evansville, IN
Slogan: A Good Judge
Brewery: 1894 – 1918
Size: 13"

Top: Square tray.
Stroh's Bohemian Beer, B. Stroh Brew-
ing Company, 1829 – 1902; The Stroh
Brewing Company, 1902 – 1919; The
Stroh Brewing Company, 1933 – present.
Annual capacity 500,000 barrels. Highest
Award and Medal, World's Fair, 1893.
Copyright: Tray by Meek Co., 1902 – 1909
Size: 13"

Bottom: Oval tray.
Stroh's Export Beer. Stroh's, Detroit,
Phone Main 316, Cleveland Branch,
396 Case Ave.
Annual capacity 500,000 barrels. Highest
Award and Medal, World's Fair, 1893
Size: 10½" x 13"

Opposite page: Circular tray.
White Rose Beer, Dallas Brewery,
Dallas, TX
Slogan: The Purest of Them All
Copyright: Kaufman & Strauss
Brewery: 1893 – 1902, 1902 – 1918,
1934 – 1939
Size: 12"

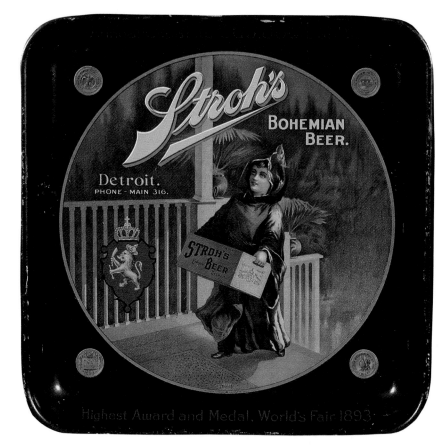

Opposite page: Oval shaped sign. King of Beer on top of the world.
Export Bottled Beer, The John Hauck Brewing Company, Cincinnati, OH
Brewery: 1881 – 1919
Size 13" x 18½"

Top: Circular tray.
Maier Brewing Company, Los Angeles, CA
Slogan: None Better, None So Pure
Brewery: 1882 – 1907, 1907 – 1971
Size: 13"

Center: Oval tray.
Kolb Bros. Brewery, West Bay City, MI
Copyright: Standard Advertising Company Coshocton
Brewery: 1888 – 1907
Size: 16½" x 13"

Bottom: Rectangle tray. Picture of the first 24 presidents. Short write-up for each president.
A & J Hochstein, Brewers, Hudson, WI
Brewery: 1893 – 1908
Size: 17¼" x 12¼"

Top: Circular tray. Spaniel dog.
Oneida Brewing Company, Utica, NY
Copyright: Litho-Chas. W. Shonk 1904
Brewery: 1884 – 1920, 1933 – 1942
Size: 12"

Bottom: Oval tray. Dixie, Doublin
Stout, Golden Drop and Silver Cream.
Manufacturing plant.
Menommee River Brewing Company,
Menominee, MI
Copyright: Standard Advertising
Company
Brewery: 1888 – 1919
Size: 16½" x 13½"

Opposite page: Circular tray. Picture
of brewery with founder's portrait on
insert. Bottles on rim.
Louis Obert Brewery, St. Louis, MO
Brewery: 1900 – 1919, 1933 – 1936
Tray by Chas. Shonk, Chicago, 1890 –
1920s
Size: 12"

LOUIS OBERT BREWERY

ST. LOUIS, U.S.A.

CHAS. W. SHONK CO. LITHO. CHICAGO.

Below: Circular tray.
Park Brewing Company, Winona, MN
Brewery: 1904 – 1920
Size: 12"

Opposite page: Oval tray.
Star Union Brewing Company, Peru, IL
Slogan: Brewers of Bottled Beer,
Keg Beer, Malt Extract and Porter
Guaranteed Pure
Copyright: The Meek Litho Company,
Chicago 1901 – 1909
Brewery: 1891 – 1920
Size: 13½" x 16½"

STAR UNION BREWING CO.

Compliments

BREWERS OF
BOTTLED BEER,
KEG BEER,
MALT EXTRACT
AND PORTER.
GUARANTEED
PURE.

PERU, ILL.

Top: Upright rectangle tray.
Stevens Point Brewing Company,
Stevens Point, WI
Brewery: 1902 – 1924
Size: 12" x 17"

Bottom: Oval tray. Inside brewery
facility.
Ropkins & Company, Hartford, CT
Slogan: Old Fashioned Ales &
Porter
The Old Fashioned Way — We
know this way is the best and our
Malt Products are brewed the old
fashioned way
Brewery: 1893 – 1920
Size: 18½" x 15"

Opposite page: Circular tray.
Beauty and the Beast.
Yuengling's, Pottsville, PA
Copyright: American Art Works 1911
Brewery: 1829 – present
Size: 13"

BEAUTY and the BEAST

113

Brewery Beauties

What can turn a man's head quicker than a beautiful woman? Probably nothing — so why not combine it with the advertising of one of their favorite beverages, *beer*. This should be a winning combination. The breweries must believe this to be true, because it's one of the most popular motifs that has been used on their advertisements.

Many trays, signs, calendars, etc. have pictured these beauties. Quite often the same beauty can be found on trays advertising different brands of beers. These are stock trays. Some were even given names by the artists or tray manufacturers. These were printed under their pictures — such as Bertha and Mildred.

Opposite page: Paper litho. Frame embossed with brewery name.
Aurora Brewing Company,
Aurora, IL
Slogan: "That Good" Aurora Beer
Brewery: 1890 – 1920, 1934 – 1939
Size: 18" x 25"

Below: Trade card. Pabst Malt Tonic,
Pabst Brewing Company, Milwaukee, WI
Brewery: 1889 – 1920, 1933 – present
Size: 7¼" x 7½"

Top: Novelty advertising item, lady's fan.
Schell's "Deer Brand," August Schell
Brewing Company, New Ulm, MN
Brewery: 1860 – present.
Size: 16½" x 8"

Bottom: Poster.
Reading Stock. Lager Ale & Porter,
P. Barbey and Son, Brewers, Reading, PA
Slogan: Celebrated Reading Stock Lager,
Ale and Porter
Brewery: 1880 – 1920
Size: 19" x 23"

Opposite page: Die cut 1903 calendar.
Embossed cardboard.
P. Barbey and Son, Brewers, Reading, PA
Slogan: Celebrated Reading Stock Lager,
Ale and Porter
Brewery: 1880 – 1920
Size: 16" x 22"

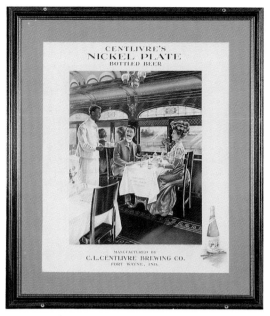

Top, left: Novelty advertising items, fans.
Left: Gluek's-Minneapolis, MN
Brewery: 1895 – 1920, 1933 – 1963
Size: 7¾" x 8¾"
Center: Tainer Brewing Company,
Philadelphia, PA
Slogan: Two popular favorites —
Franklin D. Roosevelt & Tainer Beer
Brewery: 1933 – 1937
Size: 6½" x 9"
Right: E. Robinson's Sons, Scranton, PA,
Pilsener Beer
Slogan: The Beer of Beers for over
thirty years
Brewery: 1897 – 1933
Size: 8" x 9"

Top, right: Paper sign.
Centlivre's Nickel Plate Bottled Beer.
C.L. Centlivre Brewing Company,
Fort Wayne, IN
Brewery: 1893 – 1918.
Size: 19" x 24"

Bottom: Paper sign.
Bartholomay Brewing Company,
Rochester, NY
Brewery: 1874 – 1933

Opposite page: 1904 calendar.
Cape Brewery and Ice Company,
Cape Girardeau, MO
Brewery: 1891 – 1919, 1934 – 1939
Size: 11" x 18"

Opposite page: Tin sign.
The Erie Brewing Company, Erie PA
Brewery: 1899 – 1920
Size: 23" x 33"

Top: Montage.
King's Malt Extract; tip tray with King's pure malt beer bottle — "Strengthening, good for insomnia, healthful"; Tip Tray- King's.
King's Pure Malt Department.
King's pure malt, a non-alcoholic malt extract as stated on label and tray, was used for health and strength. It was manufactured in the 1890s until the early 1930s.

Bottom: 1904 calendar.
Embossed cardboard.
The Chattanooga Brewing Company, Chattanooga, TN
Brewery: 1890 – 1915
Size: 11½" x 16"

Opposite page: Printed paper sign.
C. Gerhardt.
Slogan: Manufacturers of Brewer's
Brooms and Brushes Exclusively
Brewery: Established 1880
Size: 14" x 19"

Top: Tin sign over cardboard.
"Carnation Lady."
Grand Rapids Beer — Absolutely
Pure, Grand Rapids Brewing Company, Grand Rapids, WI (now Wisconsin Rapids, WI)
Copyright: 1908 Meek Co.
Brewery: 1905 – 1920
Size: 15" x 17"

1903 calendar.
John Gund Brewing Company,
LaCrosse, WI
Brewery: 1890 – 1920
Size: 23" x 30"

Top: Montage collection. Pilsen Brewery Company stationery pictured with fountain pen and ink holder with logo of company. Pilsen Brewing Company, Chicago, IL Letterhead date: January 20, 1939 Brewery: 1903 – 1920, 1933 – 1962

Bottom: Novelty advertising items. Right side: Thimble, Old Union Pale Beer, Union Brewing Corp., New Orleans, LA Brewery: 1911 – 1927 Size: ¾"

Middle: Sewing kit. Montgomery Brewing Company, "The Chief Beer" Montgomery, MN Brewery: 1913 – 1920, 1933 – 1942 Size: 3¾" x 5½"

Left side: Grain Belt Breweries, Minneapolis, MN Brewery: 1967 – 1975 Size: 1½" x 2¼"

Opposite page: 1901 calendar. Hamm's Brewery, St. Paul, MN Size: 19" x 24"

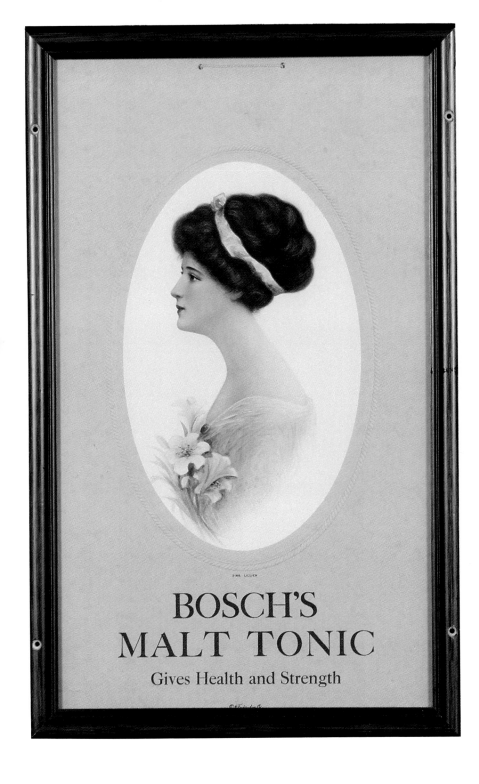

BOSCH'S
MALT TONIC
Gives Health and Strength

Opposite page: Tin sign.
O'Keefe's. Pilsner Lager. Special Extra
Mild Ale. The O'Keefe Brewery
Company, Toronto Limited
Size: 17" x 23"

Left: Printed cardboard poster.
"Lilies" from original painting by Bruno
C. Geyer for Frederickson Co.,
Art Publishers — Chicago.

Mr. Geyer was born in Germany in
1881. He attended the Art School of
Dresden. Later he moved to Berlin and
devoted his time to the painting of miniature portraits on ivory and enamel. It
is because of that training that his pictures were so wonderfully expressive.
Mr. Geyer came to America and settled
in Chicago and started his studio.

Bosch's Malt Tonic, Bosch Brewing
Company, Lake Linden, MI
Slogan: Gives Health and Strength
Brewery: 1896 – 1918, 1933 – 1934

At right: Calendar. Priscilla in middle of calendar. John Alden leading a bull on which his wife, Priscilla, is riding.
Schlitz Malt Extract, Schlitz, Milwaukee, WI
Brewery: 1858 – 1981
Size: 7" x 34"

Opposite page: Sign, embossed cardboard die cut. This sign hung in the president of the brewery's office.
Potosi Beer, Potosi, WI
Slogan: Drink Potosi Beer
Brewery: 1905 – 1920, 1933 – 1972
Size: 14½" x 19"

Top: 1903 calendar.
Stroh's Bottled, Stroh's Bottled Beer,
Detroit, MI
Slogan: America's Favorite
Size: 10" x 14"

Bottom: Jacob Moerschel, Proprietor.
Spring Brewery, St. Charles, MO
Copyright: 1900 – 1912
Size: 12" x 14"

Opposite page: Paper sign.
Roehrich & Raab Brewers, Reading, PA
Brewery 1890 – 1903
Size: 15" x 20"

Health

The Massachusetts Act of 1789 states that "the wholesome qualities of malt liquors greatly recommend them to general use, as an important means of preserving the health of the citizens of this commonwealth, and of preventing the pernicious effect of spirituous liquors."

Is Beer a "Liquid food?" "Beer has definite food value. Beer is essentially an extract or broth of cereal grains which have been first treated to render their carbohydrates soluble. Beer therefore contains most of the food values of grain products, that is — carbohydrates, minerals, and some protein. People of all times have regarded beer as a food. Their belief has been substantiated by modern science which has shown that beer contains as many nutritive elements as are found in many common foods. Beer is a beverage but, like milk, it is a food." — Dr. Howard M. Haggard, Laboratory of Applied Physiology, Practical Brewer, page 191, 1947.

Is beer a tonic? Scientists who have dispassionately analyzed beer agree that beer has a definite tonic value. Particularly, in as much as the resins of the hop have tonic effect, beer is a healthful nourishing food beverage.

In the 1600s French doctors prescribed beer for a whole range of maladies.

In a March 1986 interview in San Francisco, Nobel Prize winner, Linus Pauling, advised, "Enjoy alcohol. And enjoy it in the only right way — in moderation."

The slogan "For Health and Strength" was used quite often on old brewery advertising. Beer has always been considered healthful and nourishing, if it is consumed in moderation.

Some labels referred to it as "Liquid Bread." Tonic labels listed their many uses, some examples are, for nervous disorders, nursing mothers, good blood, problems sleeping, and "eloped mothers and distracted husbands." The breweries were eventually discouraged from using this type of advertising.

Above: Novelty advertising. (1) Letterhead — Joseph Doelger's sons, New York, 1888.
(2) Stamp holder — celluloid stamp holder, Gerhard Lang's Brewery.
Slogan: Stick to Lang's Beer and Good Health will stick to you
Brewery: 1897 – 1933
Size: 1½" x 2¼"
(3) Metal postage stamp holder.
Jos. Schlitz Brewing Company
Brewery: 1874 – 1920
Size: 1½" x 2¾"

Opposite page: 1897 calendar.
Salvador. Lager Brewers, Reinhardt & Company, Toronto, Canada
Slogan: The Life Saver
A wise merth always recommends Salvador as a beverage and strength giving restorative
Good for distracted husbands and eloped mothers
Size: 14" x 20"

Established 1872

PUBLICITY
DEPARTMENT
of the
CHICAGO ENGRAVING CO.
350 WABASH AVE. PHONE HAR.SN 623

March 23, 1907.

Du Bois Brewing Co.,
      Du Bois, Pa.
  Gentlemen:-

      We have before us your letter
of the 21st in which you state that you
have concluded to place an order for
twenty thousand booklets. We think ourselves
that it is advisable to order as large a
quanity as you can use advantageously in
order to get the lowest possible price.
We have carefully figured on the production
of twenty thousand of your booklets and
the best possible price that we can make is
($530.40) five hundred thirty dollars and
forty cents, F.O. B. Chicago.

      This is indeed an extremely low
estimate, however we are putting on the
press a similar booklet for a brewer in
Washington, D. C. and we are willing to allow
you the benefit of the saving which is
afforded by running the two booklets
together.

      Assuring you of a high class
job in every respect, we are,

      Very truly yours,

      CHICAGO ENGRAVING CO.

      Dept. of Modern Publicity.

Dic. FS-M   Mgr.

BUILDERS OF BUSINESS

BY INTELLIGENT USE OF MODERN PROMOTIONAL ADVERTISING. EXPERT ADMEN CAPABLE OF PREPARING THE MOST FORCEFUL CONVINCING BUSINESS ARGUMENTS FULL OF REASON. INDIVIDUAL SERVICE TO EACH CLIENT. WE PREPARE, WRITE, PRINT, ILLUSTRATE NEWSPAPER ADVERTISEMENTS, POSTAL CARDS, FORM LETTERS, CATALOGUES, BOOKLETS, FOLDERS, ETC. ALSO POSTERS, HANGERS, SIGNS, ETC. FOR OUTDOOR ADVERTISING.

THREE COLOR PROCESS WORK A SPECIALTY

THE MOST COMPLETE ADVERTISING, PUBLISHING, PRINTING AND ENGRAVING ESTABLISHMENT IN THE WORLD, ALL UNDER ONE ROOF

Opposite page: Paper litho sign. Pretty girl.
Wiener Export Beer and Porter, New Lebanon
Brewing Company, Lebanon, PA
Brewery: 1893 – 1920
Size: 20" x 26"

136

*Chalk statue.
Schlitz, Joseph
Schlitz Brewing
Company,
Milwaukee, WI
Brewery: 1874 –
1920, 1923 – 1981
Size: 32"*

138

Montages, Statues,
Reverse Glass

Below: Montage. Blatz 3-D statue, Blatz. Barrell man playing a banjo, singing "I'm from Milwaukee."
Size: 9½" x 16"

Sheet music. One More Mug and We'll Go Back To The Farm. Jung Brewery.

Under The Anheuser Bush. Anheuser Busch Brewery.

Cardboard sign. Kingsbury Square Dancers. "Everybody is Swinging to Kingsbury."

Backbar statues were made of plaster or chalk, therefore, they were very fragile and fortunate to have survived in one piece. A few were made of metal. The statues were placed on the backbars and were an attractive and interesting advertising piece for the beers served in the bar.

Reverse painting on glass required a great deal of hand work and was the most expensive to produce. The brilliance and depth of color is unmatched. Many of these signs contained such special features as gold or silver leaf, decals, crackled glass, stained glass, and in a few instances, inlaid mother of pearl. This form of advertising is rare, it is difficult to find in mint condition.

Top, left: Novelty advertising, candle.
Budweiser Budvar, Velke Popovice Bock 12%
Pilsner Urquell
Breweries from the Czech Republic

Top, right: Statue.
Heineken Bock.
Heineken, Amsterdam, Holland
Size: 9"

Bottom: Christmas montage.
Bottle-Lithia Christmas Beer, West Bend
Lithia Co., West Bend, WI
Sign. Adel Brau Schoen's Old Lager,
Wausau Brewing Co., Wausau, WI
Brewery: 1913 – 1920, 1933 – 1961
Size: 13½" x 16½"
Bottle. Kingsbury Christmas Brew, Kings-
bury Breweries Co., Manitowoc & Sheboy-
gan, WI

Opposite page: Montage collection.
Matchbox holder.
Size: 2¼" x 1½"
Letterhead, 1914.
Size: 8½" x 11"
Ceramic Beer Pitcher.
Size: 10½"
Atlas Beer, Panama Brewing &
Refrigerating Co.
Slogan: Don't ask for beer — Just say ATLAS

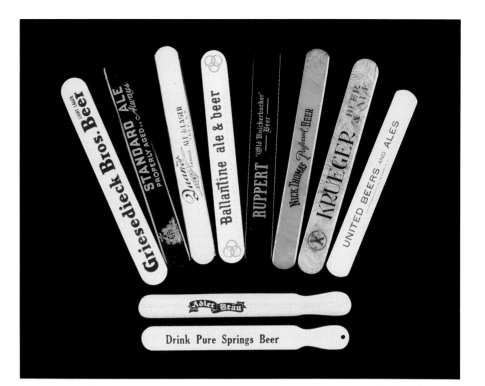

Foam Scrapers

Foam scrapers were used to clear the foam off a vessel of beer. The breweries printed their names and advertising on the scrapers and distributed them free to the bars serving their beer. They were made of plastic, metal, bone, etc. Needless to say this practice has been declared unsanitary, and they are no longer used.

Top: Foam scrapers. Left to right: (1) Griesedieck Bros. Beer (2) Standard Ale (3) Quandt Brewing Co. (4) Ballantine (5) Ruppert (6) Nick Thomas (7) Krueger (8) United Brewing Co., Newark, NJ Bottom, (9) Adler Brau (10) Springs Beer

Bottom: Novelty advertising. Cardboard barn with square dancers. Electrical dancers move. Mabel Black Label, Carling Brewing Company, Cleveland, OH Brewery: 1953 – 1971 Size: 23" x 26"

Statue. Goebel Bantam Rooster. Goebel Brewing Company, Detroit, MI Brewery: 1936 – 1964

Opposite page: Montage collection. Sports memorabilia. (1) Tray, Rheingold Salutes Gil Hodges (2) 25" long Hamm's baseball bat (3) Budweiser baseball (4) Celluloid scorekeeper, shape of baseball mitt, score runs innings (5) Blatz metal statue, 17" high (6) Baseball glove

Opposite page, top: (1) Metal statue, ice skater. Blatz, Blatz Brewing Company, Milwaukee, WI
Brewery: 1933 – 1958
Size: 15"
(2) Wooden ice skates, Prima Special, Prima Brewing Company, Chicago, IL, signed by skater, Bill Thomey
Brewery: 1938 – 1941
Size: 10"

Opposite page, bottom: Statue of hunter and deer. Bosch Beer, Bosch Brewing Company, Houghton, MI
Slogan: Refreshing as the Sportmen's Paradise!
Brewery: 1934 – 1975
Size: 12½" x 7"

Top: Statue of Bert and Harry.
Piels Real Draft, Piel Brothers, Brooklyn, NY
Slogan: You can't beat the taste of Piels Real Draft
Brewery: 1951 – 1963
Size: 11½"

Bert and Harry were created in 1955. They were on the radio and in newspapers. Their wit kept millions of New Yorkers smiling and laughing. They had a fan club which numbered over 100,000 members.

Bottom: Statue. Duck hunters with a bold duck perched in a very "safe" location.
Bosch Beer, Bosch Brewing Company, Houghton, MI
Slogan: Bosch...bright, BOLD Flavor!
Brewery: 1934 – 1975
Size: 12" x 11½"

Top: Montage (labels). Top row: (1) Highlander Pale Beer, Missoula Brewing Co., Missoula, MT, post Prohibition (2) Slinger Brand, The Storck Brewing Co., Schleisingerville, WI, pre-Prohibition (3) Old Style Select Beer, The Lima Brewing Co., Lima, OH, pre-Prohibition

Second row: (1) San Diego Beer, San Diego Brewing Co., San Diego, CA, post Prohibition (2) Dixie Beer, The Bruckmann Co., Cincinnati, OH, post Prohibition (3) Brucks Aristocrat Cereal Beverage, The Bruckmann Co., Cincinnati, OH, Prohibition (4) St. Louis Lager Beer, Anh, St. Louis, MO, pre-Prohibition

Bottom of photo: (1) Label-Storz Brewing Co., Omaha, NE, pre-Prohibition (2) Tin sign, Senate (3) Bottle, fox head (4) Label, Double Bock, Royal Brewing Co., pre-Prohibition

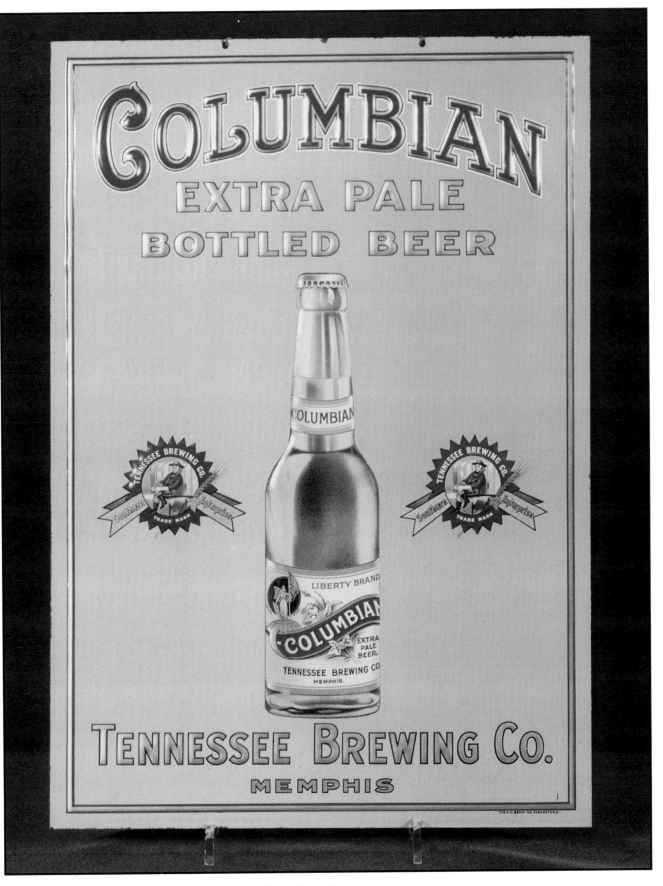

Tin sign. Bottle with Liberty brand logo. Columbian Extra Pale
Bottled Beer, Tennessee Brewing Company, Memphis, TN
H. D. Beach Co., Coshocton, OH
Brewery: 1885 – 1916, 1933 – 1955
Size: 9½" x 22"

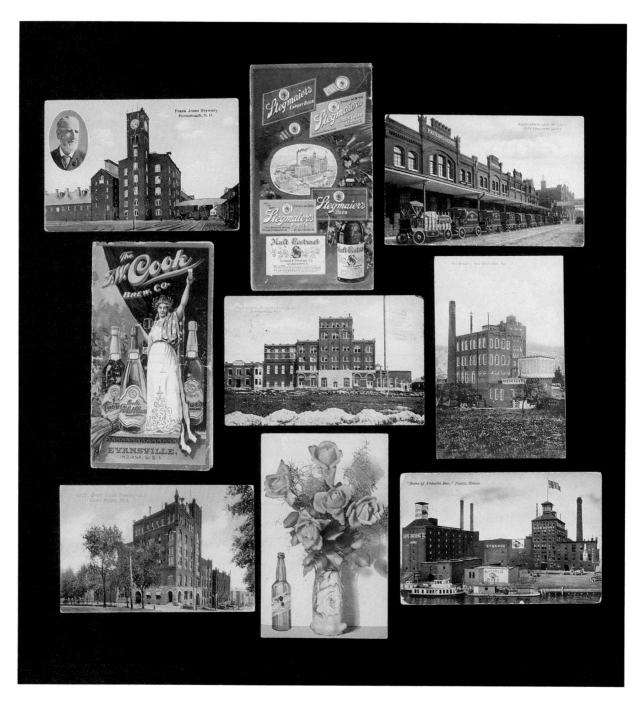

Above: Postcards and trade cards.
Top row, left: postcard, Frank Jones Brewery, Portsmouth, NH. Center: trade card, Stegmaier Brewing Co., Wilkes-Barre, PA, made by Gugler Litho Co., Milwaukee, WI. Right: postcard, Anheuser-Busch, St. Louis, MO. Middle row, left: trade card, F.W. Cook Brewing Co., Evansville," Center: postcard, Mohawk Valley Brewing Co., Schenectady, NY. Right: postcard, New Bethlehem Co., New Bethlehem, PA. Bottom row, left: postcard, Grand Rapids Brewing Co., Grand Rapids, MI. Center: trade card, Star Brewery. Right: postcard, Gipps Brewing Co., Peoria, IL.

Opposite page: Display of postcards and trade cards.

Trade Cards

In the late 1880s William Shaw, a printer of Coshocton, Ohio, was printing ads on lithographed picture cards, called advertising or trade cards. These attractive advertising media were sold to local merchants, who in turn gave them to their customers. Trade cards were collected and pasted in albums by the thousands. Today, they have found their places as desirable collectibles.

Top: Electric clock.
Keely Brewing Company, Chicago, IL
Brewery: 1878 – 1920, 1933 – 1953
Size: 12" x 16"

Bottom, right: Montage collection.
Metal sign. Fox Head Old Waukesha Ale.
Size: 9½" x 4½"

Green bottle. Fox Head Old Waukesha Ale.
Bottle. Fox Head "400" Beer.
Statue. Fox Head "400" Beer
Size: 6" x 9½"

Fox Head, Fox Head Waukesha Corp, Fox Head Brewing Company, Waukesha, WI
Fox Head "400" Beer — The "400" logo was named after a passenger train of the Chicago-Northwestern Railroad.
Brewery: 1933 – 1962

Bottom, left: Foam scrapers and holder.
Holder. Ballantine, P. Ballantine, Newark, NJ
Size: 6"

Scrapers. Ballantine, Hyde Park, Vitabrew, Yuengling
Size: 9"

Opposite page: Statue.
Gold Bond, Cleveland-Sandusky Brewing Corp., Cleveland, OH
Brewery: 1937 – 1962
Size: 15"

At right: Reverse glass corner sign.
Queen Quality/Old German Style Beer,
The Deppen Brewing Company, Reading, PA
Brewery: 1901 – 1920
Size: 13" x 25¼"

Opposite page: Reverse glass corner sign.
Lebanon, Lebanon Brewing Company,
Lebanon, PA
Brewery: 1884 – 1893
Size: 16" x 24"

Top: Miniature Brewery, Made in Germany. All copper and brass Size: 7" high

Bottom: Montage collection. Mug, Beer Drivers Union, 1913.

Sign. City Brewery, Ferd Effinger Prop., Baraboo, WI Slogan: For Health & Strength Brewery: 1911 – 1920 Size: 13½" x 16"

Tray. Hastings Brewing Company G. Kuenzel Prop. Copyright: 1911 – 1920 Brewery: 1903 – 1920 Size: 12"

Opposite page: Statue. Falstaff (bust), Falstaff Brewing Corp. Brewery: 1933 – 1958 Size: 21"

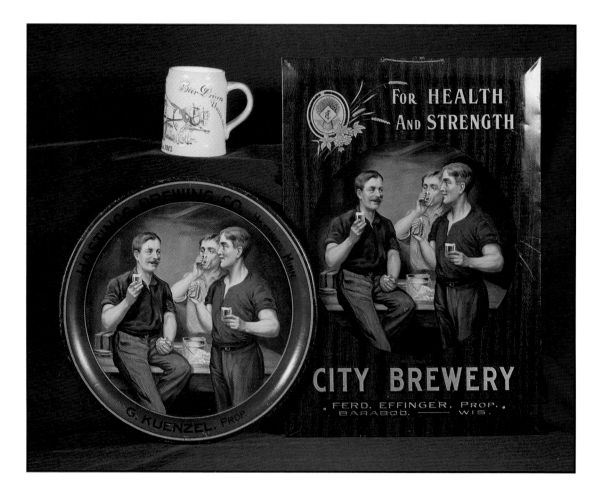

Top: Neon clock.
Old Style, G. Heileman Brewing
Co., LaCrosse, WI
Brewery: 1890 – 1962,
1962 – present

Center: Novelty advertising item.
Cigar, ash tray, cigar cutter.
Sparkling Tivoli Lager Beer, The
Springfield Brewing Company,
Springfield, MA
Brewery: 1890 – 1899
Size: 6" x 6" x 9"

Ash tray, metal. Heilman Old Style,
G. Heilman Brewing Company
Size: 7"

Cigar. Rahr's Malting Company

Bottom: Electric clock.
POC, The Pilsener Brewing Company,
Cleveland, OH
Slogan: A famous brew since 1892
A Pleasure of Course
Brewery: 1892 – 1962
Size: 14"

Opposite page: Round reverse glass corner
sign of the world.
Schlitz, Joseph Schlitz Brewing Company,
Milwaukee, WI
Slogan: Schlitz — The beer that made
Milwaukee Famous
Brewery: 1874 – 1920, 1933 – 1981
Size: 22"

Statue, plastic.
Schlitz, Joseph Schlitz Brewing Compa-
ny, Milwaukee, WI
Brewery: 1874 – 1920, 1933 – 1981
Size: 10" x 44"

Corner milk glass sign with burnished brass border.
Walter Beer, John Walter &
Company, Eau Claire, WI
Brewery: 1890 – 1915
Size: 15¼" x 20¼"

Top: Glasses. Craft Breweries.
Left: Blackstone Restaurant & Brewery, Nashville, TN
Brewery: 1994 – present
Middle: Woodstock Brewing Company, Kingston, NY
Brewery: 1991 – present
Right: Iron Horse Stout, Big River Brewing Company, Nashville, TN
Brewery: 1994 – present

Center, Top left: Match safe. Uhl's Brewery, Bethlehem, PA, during 1897
Slogan: Drink Vienna Lager
Size: 1½" x 2½"
Top right: Match safe & cigar cutter. Star Union Brewing Company, Peru, IL
Brewery: 1891 – 1920
Size: 1¼" x 2¾"
Bottom left: Match safe. Bowler Brothers Limited-Tadcaster Ale, Worchester, MA
Brewery: 1883 – 1918
Size: 1½" x 2¾"
Bottom, center: Match safe & cigar cutter. Schlitz, Schlitz Brewing Co., Milwaukee, WI
Size: 1½" x 2¾"
Bottom, right: Match safe. Bowler Bros. Brewers, Worchester, MA
Brewery: 1883 – 1918
Size: 1½" x 2¾"

Bottom: Novelty item, made during Prohibition. Blatz Grape Chewing Gum, Val Blatz Brewing Company, Milwaukee, WI
Brewery: 1911 – 1920
Size¾" x 3"

Opposite page: United States coasters.

Coasters

Most coasters were made of wood pulp, making them one of the most economical items used to advertise beer. They were usually round or square, but other unusual shapes have been discovered. Because of their reasonable cost, breweries are able to produce them for special events and change their designs often.

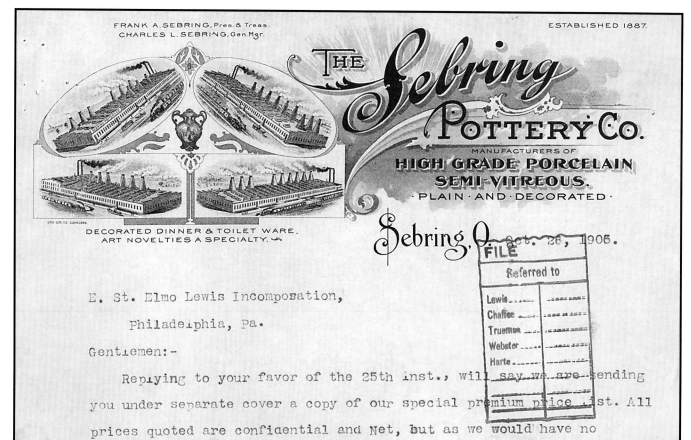

FRANK A. SEBRING, Pres. & Treas.
CHARLES L. SEBRING, Gen. Mgr.

ESTABLISHED 1887.

THE Sebring POTTERY CO.

MANUFACTURERS OF

HIGH GRADE PORCELAIN
SEMI-VITREOUS.
·PLAIN·AND·DECORATED·

DECORATED DINNER & TOILET WARE,
ART NOVELTIES A SPECIALTY.

Sebring, O. Oct. 26, 1905.

FILE

Referred to

Lewis	
Chaffee	
Trueman	
Webster	
Harte	

E. St. Elmo Lewis Incomporation,

Philadelphia, Pa.

Gentlemen:-

Replying to your favor of the 25th inst., will say we are sending
you under separate cover a copy of our special premium price list. All
prices quoted are confidential and Net, but as we would have no
Agents commission to pay we will allow you a special discount of
10% off of all net prices quoted.

We make but two shaped steins, to wit;- Queen and Tankard shapes.
We enclose herewith cut showing the Queen shape. For the Tankard
shape see page 16th of the price list. The capacity of each of these
is 10 ounces. Decorated with Monks, Ladies figures, or Fruit or
Flower Subjects with the dealers name printed in color or put on
in Gold at $3.50 per dozen. This is for any color tinting, and
the above would answer for the 3,000 premiums.

Regarding the 15 special Mugs, you would have to
stating what is wanted. It would be possible f
engraving made showing the picture of the owne
the cut of his building; in fact we make a spec
this kind, and can get up most any kind of a premi
we know what your prospective customer wants.

Why would it no do for the 15 Beer Steins for the

Mugs, Tap Markers, Cans, and Miscellaneous

Beer mugs come in many sizes and shapes. They may be plain or ornate. The mugs pictured here are rather small compared to the ones used in Europe. Many believe the reason Americans used smaller mugs is because they prefer to drink their beer much colder than Europeans. If they drank from larger mugs the beer would become warm.

These mugs were known as advertising mugs because they advertised the brewery by displaying its name and logo. Everyone was aware of what brand of beer they were drinking. These mugs were introduced in the late **1800s**.

Below: Mugs.
(1) John Gund Brewing Co., LaCrosse, WI (2) Hussa Brewing Co., Bangor, WI (3) Minneapolis Brewing Co., Minneapolis, MN (4) American Brewing Co., St. Louis, MO (5) Hagemeister Brewing Co., Green Bay, WI (6) West Bend Brewing Co., West Bend, WI (7) Michel Brewing Co., LaCrosse, WI (8) A. Fitger & Co., Duluth, MN (9) Golden Leaf/Heileman Brewing Co., LaCross, WI (10) Independent Burg Brau, Chicago, IL (11) Omaha Brewing Assn. Export Beer, Omaha, NE (12) Old Style Lager, G. Heileman, LaCrosse, WI

Mugs.

(1) *Old Times Lager, Henn & Gabler Brewery, Chicago, IL*
(2) *U. Oderbolz Brewery, Black River Falls, WI*
(3) *Becker Brewing & Milling Co., Ogden, UT*
(4) *Olympia Brewing Co., Tumwater, WA*
(5) *Belmont Brewing Co., Martin's Ferry, OH*
(6) *Monastery $5,000 Reward Guaranteed, Latrobe, PA*
(7) *Duquesne Brewing Co. Pittsburgh, PA*
(8) *The Champion Bottle & Seal Co., Cincinnati, OH*
(9) *Fred Sehring Brewing Co., Joliet, IL*
(10) *Neillsville Brewery, Neillsville, WI*
(11) *Hausman Brewing Co., Madison, WI*
(12) *Consumer's Brewery Co., Erie, PA*

PITTSBURGH, PA.

COMPLIMENTS OF
THE CHAMPION BOTTLE SEAL CO.
CINCINNATI OHIO

Fred Sehring
Brewing Co.
JOLIET.

Neillsville
Brewery
Neillsville
Wis.

Hausmann Brewing Co.

MADISON, WIS.

TRADE MARK

Consumers'
BREWING CO.
ERIE, PENN.

Below: A close up view of some of the tap markers.

Opposite page: A large display of tap markers.

166

Opposite page, top: Tap markers. Left: Hazelton Pilsener, Pilsener Brewing Co., Hazelton, PA Brewery: 1905 – 1920, 1933 – 1954 Center: Blatz Brewing Co., Milwaukee, WI Brewery: 1933 – 1958. Right: Fox head, Fox Head, Waukesha Corp., Waukesha, WI Brewery: 1933 – 1946

Opposite page, bottom: Note the Blatz Beer advertising signs behind the bar.

Top: First type of tap marker. Schlitz. Size: 3½" x 9¾"

Bottom: Tap markers. (1) Dubois Budweiser, DuBois Brewing Co., Dubois, PA (2) Meister Brau, Peter Hand Brewing Co., Chicago, IL (3) Lucky Light, General Brewing Co., San Francisco, CA (4) Schmidt Beer, Jacob Schmidt Brewing Co., St. Paul, MN (5) Tuborg, Tuborg Brewing Co., Copenhagen, Denmark (6) Piels, Piels Bro's, Brooklyn, NY (7) Old Milwaukee, Jos. Schlitz Brewing Co., San Antonio, TX (8) Pearl, San Antonio Brewing Co., San Antonio, TX (9) Stegmaier Brewing Co., Wilkes-Barre, PA (10) Red Ribbon, Mathie Ruder Brewing Co., Wasau, WI

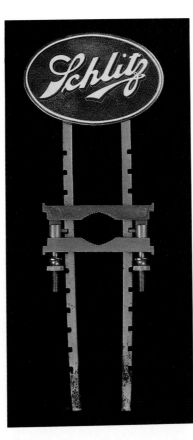

Tap Markers or Knobs

The beauty of tap handles is that they're very colorful, come in different shapes, and take up very little room in a display.

A law was passed that all tap beer must be marked with the name of the beer being dispensed from the tap. This was to assure the patron he was being served the beer he requested.

The early tap knobs were round shaped and were called ball knobs. They made very good shift knobs in cars. They were usually made of metal and plastic. The inserts, which displayed the brand, were quite often made of enamel. Most of the newer tap markers are made of a heavy plastic in many sizes and shapes. A few were made of wood or other materials.

Cans

The beer can was born in 1935. C. Krueger of Newark, NJ, was the first brewery to market beer in cans in Richmond, VA. Many other breweries followed suit.

The early problem was to convince the public that canned beer was as good as bottled. Common statements on very early beer cans were "Same as Bottle," "Same Clear Amber Color and Delicious Taste."

Also, rather detailed pictorial directions were given on the side of the can showing the customer how to open the can. In addition, a beer can opener itself was portrayed and its use explained.

A large percentage of the early beer cans were of the spout top variety. These had a pour spout and crown cap protruding from the top of the can. These cans were also called a crown or cone cans. This can lasted well into the forties, but by the early fifties it had been rendered virtually obsolete because its added height caused shelf storing and stacking difficulties. As a result of its early demise, the spout top is today the most collectible of all beer cans. In addition to the spout top, an additional indicator of old cans, as might be expected, is the thickness of the material. The older cans were much thicker and heavier than today's aluminum/tin gauge models.

Cans are one of the most difficult and challenging beer items to collect. The reason for this is, they were usually thrown away.

Photo below: Christmas beer stein. Stevens Point Beverage Co., Stevens Point, WI Brewery: 1979 – present

Photo at right: Large display of beer cans on wall.

Top photo: Beer openers.
(1) Wausau Brewing Co., Wausau, WI
Size: 4½"
(2) Slogan: Gunthers-The Word for
quality Beer, Baltimore, MD
Size: 3½"
(3) Beverwyck Beers Ales, Albany, NY
Size: 3½"
(4) Old Stock-Brown Glow, Philadelphia
Brewing Co., Philadelphia, PA
Size: 3½"
(5) Sunshine Beer-Ales, Porter. Slogan:
Have sunshine in your home — Healthful
as sunshine. Barbey Inc., established
1861, Reading, PA
Size: 3½"
(6-Angle, right side) Slogan: Call for
the brew from Kalamazoo. Kalamazoo
Brewing Company, Kalamazoo, MI
Size: 3"
(7-Angle, left side) Waldorf Ale & Lager.
Waldorf Brewing Co., Manistee, MI
Size: 4½"

Bottom photo: (1) Openers, wooden
corkscrew. Edelweiss, The Peter Schoen-
hofen Brewing Co., Chicago, IL
Brewery: 1879 – 1925
(2) Opener. Shaped like a bullet, copper
and brass. William Lemp Brewing Co.,
East St. Louis, IL
Brewery: 1920 – 1945

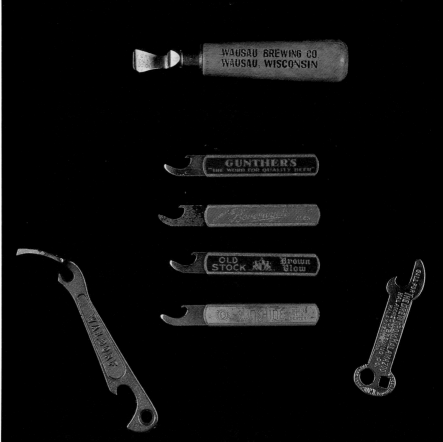

Openers

What better place for a brewery to advertise its product than on an opener? An opener's presence was always felt. Prior to the introduction of twist off tops and pull tabs, a person had to have an opener to get the contents of the beer bottle or can. Openers were kept in glove compartments, tackle boxes, lunch boxes, hung on chains from work benches and bar tops, and there was always an opener in the kitchen drawers. They were indispensable.

The first bottle opener was a corkscrew. With the introduction of the crown top in the late 1800s, bottle cap lifters and cap pullers entered the market as another advertising median. In the thirties the beer can was introduced and with it, the can piercers.

During the fifties the annual production of openers was over 200 million. Small brewers would order one quarter to one half million of the combination can piercer-cap lifter. Large breweries would order five to ten million.

In the 1960s the twist off cap and pull tab were introduced. By 1963 the bottom had fallen out of the opener market. They are becoming more collectible and rare.

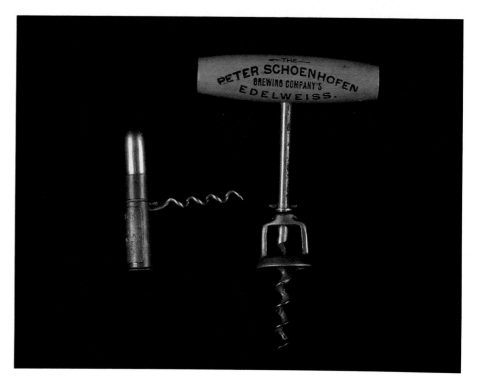

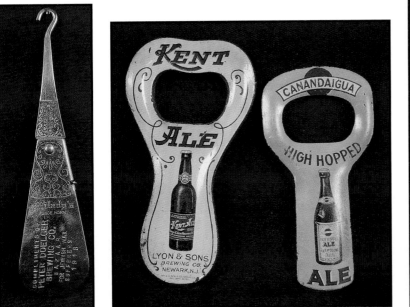

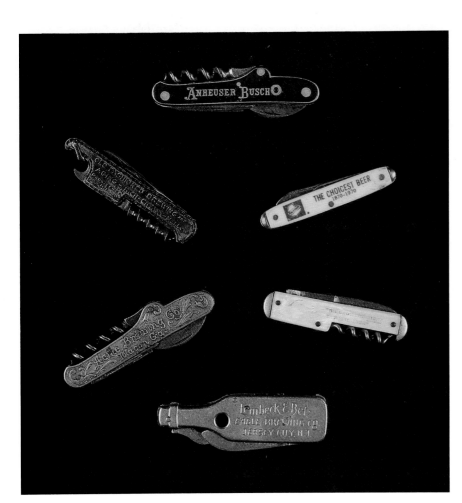

Top, left: Novelty advertisement. Shoehorn & buttonhook. Peter Doelger Brewing Company
Inscription: Bazaar for Jewish War Sufferers 1916
Size: 5" long

Top, center: Bottle openers. (1) Kent Ale, Lyon & Sons Brewing Co., Newark, NJ
Brewery: 1897 – 1920
Size: 3½"
(2) Canandaigua High Hopped Ale, J & A McKechnie Brewing Co., Canandaigua, NY
Brewery: 1895 – 1913
Size: 3½"

Top, right: Figural bottle openers. Iroquois Beverage Corp., Buffalo, NY
Brewery: 1933 – 1935
Size: 4¾"
Hauenstein Beer (shaped like a pretzel), New Ulm, MN

Bottom: Brewery advertising knives.
Top: Anheuser Busch (small hole in handle has a picture of Aldolphus Busch)
Size: 3¼"
Second row, left: Narragansett Banquet Ale, Providence, RI
Size: 3"
Second row, right: Falstaff — The choicest beer
Size: ¾"
Third row, left: ACME Brewing Co., Macon, GA
Size: 3¼"
Third row, right: Blatz — Milwaukee's first bottled beer
Size: 2¾"
Bottom: Lembeck & Betz-Eagle Brewing Co., Jersey City, NJ
Size: 3¼"

INDEX

VALUE GUIDE

Compiling a value guide is one of the most difficult parts of collecting. So many things have to be taken into consideration, such as age, rarity, and condition. All values listed in this guide are based on the memorabilia being in mint condition.

Trade card, Wm. J. Lemp
Brewing Company $75.00

Page 53
3-D shadow box, goats pulling
carriage, Minneapolis Brewing
Company ..$2,000.00 – $2,500.00

Self-framed tin sign, picnic on hill
overlooking brewery, Schmulbach
Brewing Company ....Rare

Page 54
Gold prospector, Wiedemann
Beer...............$1,000.00 – $1,200.00

Page 55
Novelty items—Pack of
cigarettes, Burkhardt
Brewing Company $75.00

Stoeckle Brewery match book..$45.00

Reading Brewery
match book $35.00

Wooden sign, Royal Flush,
Geo. Wiedemann
Brewery Company $600.00

Page 56
Self-framed tin sign, beer, cigar, and
mug on table, Buffalo Brewing
Company ..$1,200.00 – $1,500.00

Page 57
Metal Edelweiss Beer
sign....................$400.00 – $500.00

Page 58
Mug, Neillsville Brewery ....Rare

Oval tray, King Gambrinus,
August Wagner & Sons
Brewing Company $250.00

Page 60
Label ....$15.00 – $20.00

W&L Sebald sign, Middletown
Brewery $1,200.00

Page 61
Porcelain corner sign, Gambrinus
Brewing Co. ..$2,000.00 – $2,500.00

Page 62
Tin sign, Fort Pitt Beer $825.00

Page 64
Porcelain sign, Gold Label
Beer, Walter Bros.
Brewing $350.00

Porcelain sign, Horlacher's
Beer $4,500.00

Page 65
Porcelain corner sign,
Hochgreve Brewing
Company ..$2,000.00 – $2,500.00

Page 66
Tin sign, turkey with beer,
Hoster-Columbus Assoc.
Breweries Inc. $2,500.00

Page 67
Metal sign, Lucky Lager
Brewing Co. ......$300.00 – $350.00

Tin sign, two gentlemen
blowing a flute and clarinet,
Hudepohl Brewing
Company ....$600.00 – $700.00

Page 68
Tin sign, Pilsener, girl with six
pack in hand,
R. Naegeli's Sons............$225.00

Page 69
Porcelain sign, Potosi Brewing
Company ....$300.00 – $350.00

Porcelain corner sign, Princeton
Tiger Brew ..$1,500.00 – $1,800.00

Tin over cardboard, Jos. Schlitz
Brewing Company $275.00

Page 70
Tin sign, L. Schlather
Brewing Company ....Rare

Page 72
Porcelain corner sign, Geo.
Walter Brewing Co. $275.00

Oval tray, Walter Bros.
Brewing Company $475.00

Page 73
Tin sign, soldier drinking beer,
Joseph Schlitz Brewing
Company $1,500.00

Page 74
Metal sign, Jos. Schlitz Brewing
Company ....$1,200.00 – $1,400.00

Page 75
Porcelain sign, Stegmaier
Brewing Company $1,200.00

Page 76
Circular tin sign, lady holding
two bottles of beer, Blatz
Brewing Company $650.00

Page 77
Rectangle tray, Union
Brewing and Malting
Company ..$1,500.00 – $1,800.00

Page 78
Oval tray, bottle of beer and a
glass, John A.Semrad &
Bros. Brewers and
Bottlers ....$800.00 – $900.00

Page 79
Oval tray, picture of owner, John
Zynda & Sons....$600.00 – $800.00

Montage, Joseph Hensler
Brewing Co.,
Hensler's bottle.................$25.00
Hensler's tray ..$100.00 – $125.00

Page 80
Circular tray, Derby King
Beer, Southern
Breweries ......$300.00 – $350.00

Circular tray, Dubuque Beer,
Dubuque Brewing & Malting
Company ....$450.00 – $600.00

Page 81
Circular tray, Dixie Beer,
Lexington Brewing
Company $850.00

Page 82
Circular sign,
Duesseldorfer $850.00

Page 83
   Oval tray, lady holding beer,
      Excelsior Brewing
         Company ....$750.00 – $850.00

Page 84
   Circular tray, horse with nude
      holding a bottle of beer,
         Falls City Brewing............$850.00

Page 85
   Oval tin sign, lady holding bottle
      of tonic, Frank Fehr Brewing
         Company ....$850.00 – $1,000.00

Page 86
   Oval tray, Victorian lady,
      Hemrich Bros. Brewing
         Company $325.00

Page 87
   Circular tray, elf sitting on keg
      of beer, Gruenewald
         Brewery, Inc.....................$250.00

   Circular tray, Victorian lady with
      black feathers, Inland Brewing
         & Malting Company $300.00

Page 88
   Circular tray, three bottles of
      beer, Iroquois $250.00

Page 89
   Circular tray, Lackawanna
      Brewing Company $350.00

Page 90
   Circular tray, gentleman smoking
      pipe, Hanover Brewing
         Company ....$600.00 – $700.00

Page 91
   Circular tray, baby holding a
      bottle and a pipe,
         McAvoy's $450.00

Page 92
   Circular tray, Dallas
      Brewery ......$1,250.00 – $1,500.00

Page 93
   Oval tray, American flags,
      Foss-Schneider Brewing
         Company ....$800.00 – $1,200.00

Oval tray, gnomes carrying
   flagons and signs from beer
      sellers, Pabst $800.00

Page 94
   Circular tray, scenes from four
      seasons, Koppitz-Melchers
         Brewing Co. $600.00

   Montage, Pabst Blue
      Ribbon Bottles $45.00

   Foam scrapers $15.00

   Tin embossed sign ..$125.00 – $150.00

Page 95
   Calendar, twelve babies each
      holding a month of the
         year $825.00

   Trade card, Frank Fehr
      Brewing Co. $75.00

Page 96
   Oval tray, lady with a horse, The
      Home Brewing
         Company ....$500.00 – $550.00

Page 97
   Oval tray, Prima Brew,
      Independent Brewing
         Association $350.00

Page 98
   Circular tray, Hawaiian in an out-
      rigger, Honolulu Brewing &
         Malting Co...$2,000.00 – $2,500.00

Page 99
   Circular tray, beer bottle and a
      lady, Rheingold Beer,
         Voight's $400.00

Page 100
   Circular tray, beer bottle, B. Schade
      Brewing Co. ......$300.00 – $325.00

Page 101
   Circular tray, Maier
      Brewing Company $900.00

   Oval tray, Pilsener, family at
      dinner table, Grand Rapids
         Brewing Company $1,200.00

Page 102
   Rectangle tray, lady in red with
      her horse, Antigo Brewing
         Company ....$400.00 – $450.00

Page 103
   Tin sign, pennant shape,
      Sterling Brewery Inc. $150.00

   Circular tray, man pouring beer,
      Sterling Beer, Evansville
         Brewing Assoc. ..$250.00 – $300.00

Page 104
   Square tray, child carrying a case
      of beer, Stroh's Brewing
         Company ....$800.00 – $1,000.00

   Oval tray, child carrying a case of
      beer, Stroh's Brewery
         Company ....$800.00 – $1,000.00

Page 105
   Circular tray, beer bottle, glass
      and white rose, Dallas
         Brewery ....$450.00 – $550.00

Page 106
   Oval sign, King of Beer on top
      of the World, John Hauck
         Brewing Company $2,500.00

Page 107
   Circular tray, brewery, Maier
      Brewing Co.....$800.00 – $1,200.00

   Oval tray, brewery scene,
      Kolb Bros.
         Brewery ....$1,500.00 – $1,800.00

   Rectangle tray, Presidents,
      A & J Hochstein
         Brewers ....$1,000.00 – $1,200.00

Page 108
   Circular tray, Spaniel dog, Oneida
      Brewing Company $500.00

   Oval tray, manufacturing plant,
      Menommee River Brewing
         Company ..$1,500.00 – $1,800.00

Page 109
   Circular tray, brewery, Louis
      Obert Brewery ..$800.00 – $900.00

Page 110
    Circular tray, factory, Park
        Brewing Company $525.00

Page 111
    Oval tray, men playing cards and
        drinking beer, Star Union
        Brewing Co.....$400.00 – $500.00

Page 112
    Rectangle tray, man holding beer,
        Stevens Point Brewing
        Company ....$600.00 – $700.00

    Oval tray, inside brewery facility,
        Ropkins & Co. $800.00

Page 113
    Circular tray, Bulldog and a lady,
        Yuenglings ....$750.00 – $800.00

Page 114
    Litho, lady holding book, Aurora
        Brewing Company $1,500.00

Page 115
    Trade card, Pabst
        Brewing Company $55.00

Page 116
    Lady's fan, Schell's Deer
        Brand, August Schell Brewing
        Company $125.00

    Poster, Victorian girl,
        P. Barbey & Sons,
        Brewers ....$1,200.00 – $1,500.00

Page 117
    1903 Die cut calendar,lilacs
        around Victorian girl, P. Barbey
        & Sons Brewers $1,500.00

Page 118
    Novelty advertising items,
    Fans:
    Left: Glueks $125.00
    Center: Roosevelt &
        Tainer Beer $150.00
    Right: E. Robinson's
        Sons $75.00

    Paper sign, man and woman
        having dinner, C.L. Centlivre
        Brewing Co.....$650.00 – $750.00

Paper sign, Victorian lady riding a
    wheel, Bartholomay Brewing
    Company ..$1,200.00 – $1,500.00

Page 119
    1904 calendar, young nymph
        walking through water, Cape
        Brewery & Ice Co. $2,500.00

Page 120
    Tin sign, Victorian lady holding
        tray with four beers on tray,
        Erie Brewing Co. ....Rare

Page 121
    Montage collection.
    King's Malt Extract $75.00
    Tip tray with King's Pure
        Malt bottle $175.00
    Tip tray, King's-Nurse
        serving a beer $125.00

    1904 calendar, nude with two
        children, Chattanooga Brewing
        Company $950.00

Page 122
    Paper sign, young lady with scarf
        over her head,
            C. Gerhardt ....$600.00 – $800.00

Page 123
    Tin sign over cardboard, lady with
        a dozen carnations, Grand
            Rapids Brewing Co.......$1,000.00

Page 124
    1902 calendar, young girl with
        bow in hair, John Gund
            Brewing Co...$800.00 – $1,200.00

Page 125
    1903 calendar, Victorian lady with
        lilacs on shoulder, John Gund
            Brewing Co...$800.00 – $1,200.00

Page 126
    Pilsen Brewery pen and
        ink holder..........................$350.00
    Pilsen Brewing Co.
        letterhead $35.00

    Novelty advertising items:
    Thimble, Old Union Pale Beer,
        Union Brewing Co. (right) $25.00

Sewing kit, Montgomery
    Brewing Co. (center) $50.00
Grain Belt
    Breweries (left) $25.00

Page 127
    1901 calendar, lady with calendar
        pad around her, Hamm's
            Brewery ....$2,000.00 – $2,500.00

Page 128
    Tin sign, lady with flowing hair
        sitting on the moon, O'Keefe
            Brewery Company ....Rare

Page 129
    Printed cardboard poster, young
        woman with hair in bun,
            Bosch's $1,200.00

Page 130
    Calendar, Priscillia in middle,
        John Alden leading the bull his
            wife is riding, Schlitz $325.00

Page 131
    Sign, beautiful Victorian lady,
        Potosi Beer ....Rare

Page 132
    1903 calendar, sultry lady, Stroh's
        Bottled Beer..$1,500.00 – $1,800.00

    Calendar, Jacob Moerschel, Prop.,
        young lady in background,
            Spring Brewery ..$450.00 – $550.00

Page 133
    Sign, Victorian lady in chair,
        Roedrich & Raab
            Breweries ..$1,200.00 – $1,500.00

Page 134
    Novelty advertising,
        Joseph Doelger's Sons
            letterhead $35.00
    Celluloid stamp holder, Gerhard
        Lang's Brewery...............$100.00
    Metal postage stamp holder,
        Jos. Schlitz Brewing Co. ..$150.00

Page 135
    1897 calendar, ocean scene with
        lady holding Salvador
            Beer ....$2,000.00 – $2,500.00

Page 137
Sign, pretty girl, New Lebanon
    Brewing ......$1,200.00 – $1,400.00

Page 138
Chalk statue, man with Schlitz
    globe for body, Jos. Schlitz
    Brewing Company ....Rare

Page 139
Montage collection, Blatz
    Barrell man playing banjo $125.00
Sheet music, *One More Mug and
    We'll Go Back to the Farm*....$50.00
Under The Anheuser Bush $45.00
Sign, Kingsbury Square
    Dancers $75.00

Page 140
Novelty advertising
    candle, Breweries from Czech
    Republic $25.00

Ram statue, Heineken $150.00

Montage, Lithia Christmas
    Beer, West Bend Lithia Co. $5.00
Kingsbury Christmas
    Brew, Manitowoc
    & Sheboygan $5.00
Adel Brau Schoen's
    sign $50.00

Page 141
Montage, Panama Brewing &
    Refrigerating Company
Match box holder $65.00
Letterhead $25.00
Ceramic beer pitcher $250.00

Page 142
Foam scrapers,
    Griesedieck $35.00
    Standard Ale $26.00
    Quandt Brewing....................$85.00
    Ballantine.............................$10.00
    Ruppert $15.00
    Nick Thomas $75.00
    Krueger $25.00
    United Brewing $75.00
    Adler Brau $40.00
    Springs Beer $55.00

Mabel Black Label cardboard barn
    Carling Brewing Co. $250.00

Goebel Bantam Rooster, Goebel
    Brewing Co. ......$100.00 – $125.00

Page 143
Montage collection
Tray, Rheingold salutes
    Gil Hodges...........................$45.00
Hamm's baseball bat $25.00
Budweiser baseball $10.00
Celluloid scorekeeper
    (baseball mitt shape) $100.00
Blatz Metal statue $150.00
Baseball glove $125.00

Page 144
Blatz Ice Skater statue, Blatz
    Brewing Co. ......$100.00 – $125.00
Wooden Ice Skates (signed by Bill
    Thomey), Prima
    Brewing Co. $500.00

Statue, duck hunter and deer
    Bosch Brewery Co. $475.00

Page 145
Statue, Bert & Harry,
    Piel Bros. ....$75.00 – $125.00

Statue, duck hunter with
    bold duck, Bosch
    Brewery Company............$475.00

Page 146
Labels,
    Highlander Pale....................$35.00
    Slinger Brand.......................$55.00
    Old Style Select $75.00
    San Diego $30.00
    Dixie $35.00
    Brucks $40.00
    St. Louis Lager $75.00
    Storz $85.00
Tin sign, Senate $60.00
Bottle, Fox Head $10.00
Label, Double Bock
    Royal Brewing Co................$75.00

Page 147
Tin sign, beautiful bottle with
    Liberty Brand logo, Tennessee
    Brewing Co..................$175.00

Page 148
Post card, Frank Jones
    Brewery $35.00

Trade card, Stegmaier
    Brewing Co. $60.00
Post card, Anheuser
    Busch $35.00
Trade card, F.W. Cook
    Brewing Co........................$35.00
Post card, Mohawk Valley
    Brewing Co........................$50.00
Post card, New
    Bethlehem Co.....................$50.00
Post card, Grand Rapids
    Brewing Co........................$40.00
Trade card, Star
    Brewery Co........................$50.00
Post card, Gibbs
    Brewing Co........................$35.00

Page 150
Electric clock, Keely
    Brewing Co.........................$450.00

Foam scrapers,
    Ballantine............................$10.00
    Hyde Park $20.00
    Vitabrew $30.00
    Yuengling............................$25.00
P. Ballantine holder $100.00

Montage collection
Metal sign, Fox Head Old
    Waukesha $150.00
Green bottle, Fox Head Old
    Waukesha $15.00
Bottle, Fox Head "400" Beer ..$15.00
Statue, Fox Head $125.00

Page 151
Statue, Gold Bond, Sandusky
    Brewing Corp. $575.00

Page 152
Reverse glass corner sign,
    Queen Quality, Deppen
    Brewing Co. $850.00

Page 153
Reverse glass corner sign
    Lebanon Brewing
    Company ..$1,200.00 – $1,400.00

Page 154
Miniature Brewery $250.00

Montage collection,
    Mug, Beer Drivers Union $75.00

Sign, City
Brewery ......$800.00 – $1,200.00
Tray, Hastings Brewing
Company ....$800.00 – $900.00

Page 155
Statue, Falstaff Brewing
Company $350.00

Page 156
Neon clock, Old Style,
G. Heileman
Brewing Company $650.00

Novelty advertising items,
Cigar cutter,
Sparkling Tivoli $550.00
Ash tray, G. Heileman
Brewing Company $50.00
Cigar, Rahr's Malting
Company $5.00

Clock, Pilsener
Brewing Company $225.00

Page 157
Reverse glass corner sign of
world, Jos. Schlitz Brewing
Company ..$1,800.00 – $2,000.00

Page 158
Statue holding light, plastic world/
globe, Joseph Schlitz Brewing
Company $275.00

Page 159
Glass sign, Walter Beer, John
Walter & Co. $950.00

Page 160
Glasses, Blackstone
Restaurant & Brewery $5.00
Woodstock Brewing Co.............$5.00
Iron Horse Stout, Big River
Brewing Company $5.00

Uhl's Brewery........................$200.00
Match safe & cigar cutter, Star
Union Brewing Co. $175.00
Match safe, Bowler Bros. Ltd ..$125.00
Match safe, Schlitz
Brewing Co........................$100.00
Match safe, Bowler Bros.
Brewers $125.00
Blatz Gum ....$50.00 – $75.00

Page 163
John Gund Brewing Co.........$200.00
Hussa Brewing Co. $500.00
Minneapolis Brewing Co. $90.00
American Brewing Co. $185.00
Hagemeister Brewing Co. $175.00
West Bend Brewing Co........$165.00
Michel Brewing Co. $300.00
A. Fitger & Co. ....Rare
Golden Leaf/Heileman
Brewing Co.......................$250.00
Independent Burg Brau $125.00
Omaha Brewing Assn. $200.00
Old Style Lager $200.00

Page164
Mugs,
Old Times Lager $275.00
U. Oderbolz ....Rare
Becker Brewing $400.00
Olympia Brewing $125.00
Belmont Brewing $175.00
Monastery $150.00
Duquesne Brewing $175.00
Champion Bottle
& Seal............................$35.00
Fred Sehring
Brewing $135.00
Neillsville
Brewing ....Rare
Hausman
Brewing Co. $450.00
Consumer
Brewing $140.00

Page 168
Hazleton Pilsener
tap marker ....$75.00 – $100.00

Blatz tap marker.....................$45.00

Fox Head $35.00

Page 169
Schlitz tap
marker ....$200.00 – $250.00

Tap markers,
Dubois-Budweiser $50.00
Meister Brau $10.00
Lucky Light $5.00
Schmidt $5.00
Tuborg $5.00
Piels.....................................$5.00
Old Milwaukee $25.00

Pearl $25.00
Stegmaier $25.00
Red Ribbon $50.00
Mug, Oldenberg Brewery........$20.00

Page 170
Christmas Beer Stein, Stevens
Point Brewery Company $35.00

Page 172
Openers,
Wausau Brewing $65.00
Gunthers $40.00
Beverwyck $40.00
Old Stock Brown
Glow $45.00
Sunshine $40.00
Kalamazoo
Brewing $65.00
Waldorf $65.00

Openers,
Wooden corkscrew $100.00
William Lemp
Brewing Co.
(bullet shaped) $100.00

Page 173
Shoehorn &
Buttonhook $300.00

Bottle openers,
Kent Ale $65.00
Canandaigua High
Hopper $65.00

Bottle openers, Iroquois
(Indian shaped) $35.00
Hauenstein Beer
(pretzel shaped) $38.00

Brewery advertising knives,
Anheuser Busch $200.00
Narragansett
Banquet Ale $75.00
Falstaff................................$75.00
ACME $175.00
Blatz $75.00
Lembeck & Betz $150.00

Omaha Brewing Association Employees and Owners Company Picture.
When the brewery employees and owners posed for the company pictures they usually displayed some of their advertising, such as the corner signs shown in this picture. As we collectors view these old pictures we dream of finding some of these pieces of memorabilia. They also had kegs of their products and some employees were usually enjoying the fruits of their hard labor.

Schroeder's ANTIQUES Price Guide

. . . is the #1 best-selling antiques & collectibles value guide on the market today, and here's why . . .

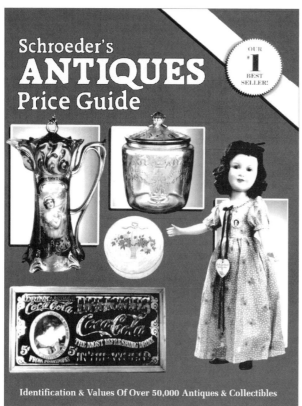

Schroeder's ANTIQUES Price Guide

OUR #1 BEST SELLER!

Identification & Values Of Over 50,000 Antiques & Collectibles

8½ x 11, 608 Pages, $12.95

- *More than 300 advisors, well-known dealers, and top-notch collectors work together with our editors to bring you accurate information regarding pricing and identification.*

- *More than 45,000 items in almost 500 categories are listed along with hundreds of sharp original photos that illustrate not only the rare and unusual, but the common, popular collectibles as well.*

- *Each large close-up shot shows important details clearly. Every subject is represented with histories and background information, a feature not found in any of our competitors' publications.*

- *Our editors keep abreast of newly developing trends, often adding several new categories a year as the need arises.*

If it merits the interest of today's collector, you'll find it in *Schroeder's*. And you can feel confident that the information we publish is up to date and accurate. Our advisors thoroughly check each category to spot inconsistencies, listings that may not be entirely reflective of market dealings, and lines too vague to be of merit. Only the best of the lot remains for publication.

Without doubt, you'll find
SCHROEDER'S ANTIQUES PRICE GUIDE
the only one to buy for
reliable information and values.

COLLECTOR BOOKS
A Division of Schroeder Publishing Co., Inc.